WORLD RELIGIONS

BENSON Y. LANDIS is Editor of the *Yearbook of American Churches* and Editor of Research Publications of the National Council of Churches of Christ in the United States of America. He has long been a participant in interdenominational cooperation, is a student of Roman Catholicism and contributor to Roman Catholic periodicals, and was one of the first promoters of the National Conference of Christians and Jews. A graduate of Moravian College, he holds a Ph.D. from Columbia University, an L.H.D. from Moravian, and an LL.D. from St. Francis Xavier University.

WORLD RELIGIONS was first published in 1957.

WORLD RELIGIONS

A Brief Guide to the Principal Beliefs and Teachings
of the Religions of the World and to the Statistics
of Organized Religion

by

BENSON Y. LANDIS

A Dutton *Paperback*

NEW YORK

E. P. DUTTON & CO., INC.

.

Library of Congress Catalog Card No.: 57-5344

CONTENTS

CONTENTS

INTRODUCTION

THIS IS A concise description of the main religions of the world. It contains summaries of many available writings by leaders of the various religions and draws from numerous other sources listed below.

World Religions provides information on the beliefs and teachings of religions, their history, and available statistics. The aim is to provide a fair interpretation of the emphases in these many religious bodies, without any attempt to pass judgment.

Statistical information has generally been "rounded" because this is a brief guide for persons with many backgrounds and interests, and not a technical, statistical manual. Probably you remember rounded figures more readily than those presented in precise detail, and probably can compare such figures more easily. It must be stated altogether frankly that the more global the figures the less reliable they are because of varied methods of compilation and the necessity for combining estimates in certain nations with careful statistical reporting in others. And in the Far East, as is reported in the pages that follow, many people are adherents to more than one religion.

Much widely scattered information has been assembled and digested. So far as possible the language is that of the layman. The author is a layman, not a theologian, but enough of a student of the theologies of the world to realize that many ideas cannot be simplified no matter how simple the words that are used. Many religious teachings are difficult to understand and to explain. A glossary listing a number of technical terms is included on pp. 143-47.

Throughout this book special attention is paid to statistical information from the English-speaking world, with emphasis on materials about the United States, Great Britain, and Canada.

An alphabetical arrangement, with cross referencing, and an index, has been employed with the aim of making the book valuable for varied reading and reference.

A Classification of Religious Bodies

Recognizing that no one classification of religious bodies can be completely satisfactory in all nations, a brief one is given here as a general guide to the groups and bodies which are later described in *alphabetical order* without regard to major classifications.

Baha'ism
Buddhism
Christianity
  Anglicans
  Eastern Orthodox Churches
  Protestants
    Adventists
    Baptists
    Brethren
    Church of Christ, Scientist (Christian Science)
    Churches of God
    Churches of the New Jerusalem (Swedenborgian)
    Congregationalists

Disciples of Christ
Ethical Culture Movement
Evangelistic Associations
Friends
Jehovah's witnesses
Latter-day Saints (Mormons)
Lutherans
Mennonites
Methodists
Moravians
Old Catholics
Pentecostal
Presbyterians
Reformed
Salvation Army
Spiritualists
Unitarians
Universalists
Roman Catholics
Confucianism
Hinduism
Islam
Jainism
Judaism
Shintoism
Taoism
Zoroastrianism

Although writings of thorough scholars have been drawn upon, this is not a scholar's book on comparative religion. It is rather for general readers, students, libraries, professional workers and others who need a short and accessible source book on a variety of topics.

NOTE ON SOURCES

WCH. *World Christian Handbook*, London, 1952, presents a compilation of figures reported by Christian bodies throughout the world. In *World Religions*, reference is particularly made to figures reported for Great Britain and nations other than the United States.

YBAC. These initials note a reference to recent statistical information reported by the many religious bodies in continental United States to the *Yearbook of American Churches*, published annually by the National Council of Churches, New York.

CRB. Much use for historical purposes has been made of a public document now out of print. This is *Religious Bodies, 1936*, Vol. I and II, Washington, U.S. Department of Commerce, Bureau of the Census, 1941. These volumes contain valuable statements approved by historians and officials of most of the religious bodies of the United States, with data on the European origin of many of these. Thus the initials CRB (Census of Religious Bodies) are frequently inserted in the text to indicate that certain material comes from that source.

For the various religions a great many sources have been consulted. Among these the following may be noted here:

The Eleven Religions and Their Proverbial Lore. A

Comparative Study by Selwyn Gurney Champion. New York, E. P. Dutton and Co., 1945. A symposium mainly by English scholars.

The World's Religions. By Charles Samuel Braden. Nashville, Abingdon Press, 1954 (Rev. Ed.).

The Essence of Judaism. By L. Baeck. London, The Macmillan Company, 1936.

The Great Religions of the Modern World. Edited by Edward J. Jurgi. Princeton, N.J., Princeton University Press, 1947.

Questions to a Moslem: An Exposition of Islam. By Mohammed El-Zayyat. Washington, Egyptian Embassy, 1954.

WORLD RELIGIONS

I

DESCRIPTIONS OF RELIGIONS

ADVENTISTS. In the early Christian Church it was commonly held that the return of Christ to the earth was near, and that this second advent would give divine completion to the history of this world. Today, members of a number of religious bodies believe in the physical return of Jesus Christ.

The largest denomination of this specific group of believers is the Seventh-day Adventist, with 3,500 members in 1863, and 925,000 at present. Of the latter, more than 275,000 are in North America; 46,000 in northern Europe; 115,000 in South Africa; 70,000 in South America; the others in nearly all other sections of the world. (*Seventh-day Adventist Yearbook, Washington, D.C., 1955.*)

Historical Notes. In America and elsewhere, the 1840's were distinguished for a number of religious awakenings, one of which was the growing conviction among students of Biblical prophecy that the second coming of Christ was drawing near. This belief resulted in great stirrings among people in Britain, on the continent of Europe, and in North America. The historian Thomas B. Macaulay noted in 1829 that many who held to the doctrine of the second coming were distinguished by rank wealth, and ability. It was estimated then that some 700 clergymen of the Church of England were part of this "awakening."

Christians of many denominations in America were interested in the movement for second advent evangelism. Two prominent leaders were the Rev. Joshua V. Himes, of Boston, and William Miller, a Baptist layman of New Hampton, N.Y. From among those identified with the Adventists engaged in this movement there arose a small group in Washington, N.H., in 1844, who began to observe the seventh day as the Sabbath, and who believed in the imminent, personal second advent of Christ.

William Miller (1782-1849), a farmer and a captain in the War of 1812, was a diligent student of the Scriptures. As a result of his studies, he believed not only that the advent was at hand but also that the date could be fixed with some definiteness. He confidently expected that Christ would return some time between March 21, 1843, and March 21, 1844. When the Lord did not return in the spring of 1844, Mr. Miller published his mistake.

By 1845, it was reported that there were about 1,000 local churches in many denominations which were adventist. Out of a general conference held at Albany came several American adventist denominations.

The persons who met at Washington, N.H., did not originally use the term Seventh-day Adventist. By 1860 the denominational name was assumed and a publishing house established at Battle Creek, Michigan. In 1903, the headquarters was moved to Takoma Park, Washington, D.C. Meanwhile, sanitariums were built and missionaries were sent abroad.

Principal Beliefs and Doctrines. The numerous official doctrines include the following:

The Holy Scriptures are the rule of faith and practice. The Godhead, the Trinity, consists of the Eternal

Father, the Son of the Eternal Father, the Holy Spirit.

Jesus Christ is very God. While retaining his divine nature, He took upon Himself the nature of the human family, died for our sins, rose from the dead, and in heaven ever lives to make intercession for us.

Baptism of believers by immersion.

The new birth, through faith, by the re-creative power of God.

Immortality and eternal life come to redeemed man only as a free gift in Christ; and "this mortal shall put on immortality" at the second coming of Christ.

The believer will be led to abstain from all intoxicating drinks, tobacco, and narcotics.

Gospel work is to be supported by the Scriptural plan of tithes and offerings.

The second coming of Christ is the hope of the church. Attention must be called to the signs of the times. While no man knows the day or hour, prophecy has given signs. The ministry of Jesus in heaven, before he comes, is a work of judgment which will determine between the just and the unjust. Seventh-day Adventists believe it is their duty to carry that message to every people and tongue.

Form of Worship. The Sunday service is a relatively informal one, consisting of hymns, reading of Scripture, prayer, sermon, offering.

Form of Organization. The local church is largely self-governing but under the supervision of the conference of which it is a member. An effort is made to collect a specific sum each week from every member for foreign missions. The support of the ministry comes through the tithing system, whereby each member is expected to contribute one-tenth of his income. The conference pays the minister's salary.

Foreign missions are active over the entire world, in many languages. Over 7,300 missionaries have been sent out by the denomination. The denomination has built numerous hospitals and has disseminated much information regarding healthful living and temperance. Its sanitariums are well-known. Many of the Adventists are vegetarians. An extensive publishing enterprise is carried on (CRB).

ADVENT CHRISTIAN CHURCH. This body dates from 1855, when followers of an Adventist leader, Jonathan Cummings, separated from others in the adventist movement, holding that immortality is the gift of God to be bestowed in the resurrection on the true followers of Christ. Baptism is by immersion. Baptism and the Lord's supper are the sacraments recognized. Women and men are eligible to office in the church. Local churches are congregational in government, but a district conference ordains the ministers. Home and foreign missions are promoted. It recently reported over 35,000 members. It maintains an office in Aurora, Ill. (YBAC).

AMISH, *see Mennonites*

ANGLICANS. There are fourteen separate churches of the Anglican communion, united with each other by a common tradition of faith, church order, and worship. Their total constituency is over 30,000,000 persons, throughout the world (WCH).

The separate churches of the Anglican communion are:

The Church of England
The Church in Wales
The Church of Ireland

The Episcopal Church in Scotland
The Protestant Episcopal Church in the U.S.A.
The Anglican Church in Canada (formerly Church of England in Canada)
The Church of India, Pakistan, Burma and Ceylon
The Church of England in Australia and Tasmania
The Church of the Province of New Zealand
The Church of the Province of South Africa
The Church of the Province of the West Indies
The Nippon Sei Ko Kwai
The Chung Hua Sheng Kung Hui
The Church of the Province of West Africa

The Protestant Episcopal Church reports 2,750,000 members in the United States (YBAC). The Church of England reports 2,965,200 persons on the electoral rolls, and 1,948,215 Easter communicants (WCH). The Canadian government census (1951) reports 2,060,000 persons in the Church of England in Canada, now the Anglican Church of Canada.

Historical Notes. This world-wide communion developed from the Church of England. The separation of this church from the Roman Catholic Church came about in a long series of changes. Generally, the break is associated with King Henry VIII, who established for himself "the headship" of the church in 1534.

The Act of Supremacy of that year acknowledged the King as "the only supreme head on earth of the Church of England." In early years, the Reformation in England was one of policy, not of doctrine. The monasteries were suppressed. By 1549 certain Protestant doctrines were accepted, and the first book of Common Prayer was adopted. The national church retained much of its continuity with early Christian institutions of Britain. It retained, for example, much of the ritual of the early church. The Church of England is known as an "established" church (established by law), or a "state church."

The expansion of this church to other parts of the world took place along with commercial adventures and expeditions of discovery of the English people. While the Church of England remains an established or state church, its sister churches are not. But all distinguishing characteristics of the Church of England are found throughout the world—the standards, sacraments, ministry, and membership in the Lambeth Conference, London, a body for exploration and discussion of common interests.

Principal Beliefs and Doctrines. The Anglican communion doctrine is comprehensive, founded on the Scripture. The three creeds—Apostles', Nicene, and Athanasian —express for Anglicans their sense of the Scripture.

These three creeds are among the historically important summaries or symbols of basic doctrines of Christian faith. The Apostles' Creed was once called the old Roman symbol. It begins: "I believe in God the Father Almighty, creator of heaven and earth. And in Jesus Christ. . . ." Its present form appeared about the year 650. It is much used by many Protestant bodies and by the Roman Catholic Church. It contains the line "He descended into hell" (or darkness), which is omitted from the creed called Nicene. In the Apostles' Creed is found the words "resurrection of the body," which is written "of the dead" in the Nicene Creed.

The Nicene Creed begins: "I believe in One God the Father Almighty, maker of heaven and earth, and of all things visible and invisible, and in One Lord Jesus Christ. . . ." This is usually regarded as a revision made by the first Council of Constantinople, in 381, of a creed adopted at Nicea, 325, although there is evidence that it was written earlier by St. Cyril in Jerusalem. The Nicene is used by Roman Catholic, Anglican, and certain Protestant churches.

The Athanasian Creed is an elaborate statement on the Trinity and the Incarnation. It is now generally believed that it was not written by St. Athanasius (c. 298-373), but by a sixth century author. It is used by Roman Catholic and Anglican churches, but not by the Protestant Episcopal Church in the United States (see below).

The Articles of Religion are understood to give expression to matters less fundamental and deal in large part with pronouncements on issues that excited controversy several hundred years ago, certain of which no longer engage public interest. The articles date from Elizabeth's reign and were written by a group of bishops. Theologically they are regarded as mainly Calvinistic in emphasis. They repudiate certain Roman teachings, e.g., those on purgatory. They declare that the only two sacraments ordained by Christ are those of baptism and the Lord's supper.

The Catechism is a book of instruction to be learned by the persons brought before a Bishop to be confirmed. It is a series of questions and answers for the purpose of teaching a religious system, including the significance of the sacraments of baptism and holy communion.

In the baptism of children, pouring or immersion is allowed. For those not baptized in infancy, baptism may also be by the form preferred. For those baptized, reception is by confirmation by the Bishop, after instruction in history, worship, and doctrine.

Spokesmen allege that the Anglican communion stands for the historic Christian religion in full, with all of its emphases. It is a sort of family of provinces or dioceses aware of the family connections.

There are "party" divisions in the Anglican communion, as in other religious bodies. In the first half of the nineteenth century the Oxford Movement in England led to emphasis on Roman Catholic traditions. The successors of this group are known as the high church party. The low church, or evangelical party, stresses Protestant traditions. Broad church adherents generally follow a middle course; certain of these are also called "rationalists."

Development in U.S.A. At the close of the American Revolution, Anglican churches in the colonies were somewhat disorganized. Several efforts at organizing resulted in a union of the different forces, in 1789, when a general convention was held and a constitution and Book of Common Prayer were adopted. Thus the Protestant Episcopal Church was constituted in the same year that the federal government was completely organized. In 1792 the first Bishop was consecrated in America.

Growth was slow. In the new nation, the Protestant Episcopal Church was regarded by many as only an English institution. Expansion came and confidence was gained as opinion changed. In 1817, the General Convention set up the General Theological Seminary, in New York, and in 1820, the Domestic and Foreign Missionary Society. New bishops moved into the West as people settled in this vast unoccupied region. The number of rectors in Virginia increased from five in 1814 to nearly one hundred in 1841. Later, in spite of the strains of the American Civil War, the Protestant Episcopal Church retained its unity.

The Protestant Episcopal Convention of 1789 rejected the Athanasian Creed. Thus the doctrinal symbols of the

Church in the United States are the Apostles' and Nicene creeds. The convention also accepted with modifications the Articles of the Church of England. In 1919 the church created a National Council, in New York, which conducts the national work of the body between the Triennial Conventions.

Form of Organization. The local parish has as its officers: a rector; wardens, usually two; and vestrymen who are trustees and hold the property. Dioceses are generally organized on state lines and are governed by a convention whose members are the clergy of the local parishes and at least one lay delegate from each parish. Sections of states not organized into dioceses are established by the House of Bishops and the General Convention as missionary districts. These districts may be elevated into dioceses or made parts of existing dioceses.

The General Convention, the highest ecclesiastical authority, consists of two Houses, the House of Bishops and the House of Deputies. The latter consists of elected clergymen and lay delegates. The Convention meets every three years and does much of its business in the general manner of that of the Congress of the United States. The ecclesiastical head of the Protestant Episcopal Church is the Presiding Bishop, who is elected by the General Convention.

There are three orders in the ministry: bishops, priests, and deacons. After serving a year, a deacon twenty-four or more years of age may be ordained to the priesthood. A bishop is a priest elected to that office by a diocesan convention, subject to approval by the majority of the standing committees of the dioceses and a majority of the bishops in the United States.

Form of Worship. The churches of the Anglican communion are known as liturgical in their form of worship. Thus, in the Protestant Episcopal Church in the United States, the *Book of Common Prayer* contains the order for Holy Communion, the Order for Morning Prayer, and the Litany, which "are the regular services appointed for public worship in this Church, and shall be used accordingly." The minister may in addition at his discretion "use other devotions taken from this book." In certain circumstances, with ecclesiastical permission, "such other devotions as aforesaid may be used, when the edification of the Congregation so requires, in place of the order for Morning Prayer, or the Order for Evening Prayer."

BAHÁ'ÍS. The Bahá'í faith is that begun by Bahā'u'llāh (1817-92). Its followers regard it as a universal religion, or a teaching of the unity of all religions. It originated in Persia in 1844, from which country its followers were recently expelled. It is reported to be organized in some 200 countries and colonies and divisions of nations. In the U.S.A. there are about 1,300 groups with some 5,000 members, according to *The Handbook of Denominations,* New York, 1955.

Historical Notes. Out of Islam in the 1840's came Babism, a movement led by Mirza Ali Muhammed, who took the title of the Bab, meaning Gate or Door. He was executed in 1850. One of his main supporters was Mirza Husayn Ali (1817-92), known as Bahā'u'llāh, meaning Glory of God. He was exiled from Baghdad in 1852. First conceived as a reform movement within Islam, the movement added elements from Christianity and other religions.

Principal Beliefs and Doctrines. This religion emphasizes the oneness of mankind. Believers say that spiritual power has been given to mankind which expresses itself in a desire for unity. The founder gave this statement of principles.

"Unfettered search after truth and the abandonment of all superstition; the oneness of mankind—all are 'leaves of one tree, flowers in one garden'; religion must be a cause of love and harmony, else it is no religion; all religions are one in their fundamental principles; religion must conform with science, bringing faith and reason into full accord; and recognition of the unity of God and obedience to His commands as revealed through His Divine Manifestations. . . ."

Form of Worship. Believers and inquirers meet at intervals for study of the "Revealed Words." The religion forbids the appointment of professional clergy. It is held that spiritual instruction should not be done for pay. In the U.S.A., there is a national center at Wilmette, Ill., where there will be a sanctuary for prayer and praise.

Form of Organization. In order to become a voting member of a local group or community or assembly one must be a resident of the place in which the group meets, be twenty-one years of age, and have received the approval of the local assembly that he possesses the necessary qualifications. The movement has no ecclesiastical organization. Each local assembly has nine members. The local assemblies then elect nine persons who become the governing body of the National Spiritual Assembly. In the symbolism of this religion, nine is the number of perfection.

BAPTISTS. The Baptist World Alliance brings together representatives of Baptists from sixty nations. Baptist bodies in the world have a total constituency of 40,000,000 persons. (WCH) The Baptist Union of Great Britain and Ireland reports 335,640 members. (WCH) In the United States, twenty-six Baptist denominations have 18,800,000 members. (YBAC) In Canada the government census of 1951 reported 520,000 Baptists. The office of the Baptist World Alliance is in Washington, D.C.

Certain statements issued at a session of the Baptist World Alliance, London, 1955, sum up emphases of Baptists throughout the world:

"Churches must be free from the interference of the states, and all churches should, as far as their principles permit, abide by the laws of the state.

"Real religious liberty guarantees not only freedom to worship . . . but to teach, preach, publish, and advocate openly.

"Toleration is not enough. Freedom to worship is not enough. As Baptists, we seek to be accepted everywhere as equals in Christ, with all the privileges and responsibilities of loyal citizens.

"The right to be free is a gift from God to all men of whatever race, and . . . a person is not born into a religious faith.

"A man's right to choose or change his faith must be preserved as well as his liberty to dissent."

It is a distinct tenet of Baptists that they acknowledge no human founders of their church, "recognize no human authority," and subscribe to no human creed. For all these, Baptists go to the New Testament. There is no historian who can trace precisely a succession of Baptist churches over the centuries. Baptists believe that in every Christian age there have been effective witnesses to Baptist principles.

Historical Notes. After the Reformation, in the early

part of the sixteenth century, Anabaptists (re-baptizers) appeared in Switzerland and Germany. They were convinced that persons baptized in infancy must, upon later profession of their faith, be baptized again to gain admission to full church membership. In spite of severe opposition by both Protestant and Roman Catholic churches, the Anabaptists grew in numbers. Some were driven from Germany into the Low Countries and there gathered under the leadership of Menno Simons (see Mennonites). To the influence of these people, English Baptists owe their first churches. About 1640, a group in England became convinced from a study of the New Testament that the apostolic form of baptism was by immersion.

The first Baptist Churches in America were the one established by Roger Williams, known as an apostle of religious liberty, in 1639 in Providence, R.I., and that in Newport, R.I., organized by Rev. John Clarke in 1638. Roger Williams had been banished from the Massachusetts Colony in 1631 because "he broached and divulged new and dangerous opinions against the authority of magistrates." When settled in Providence, he taught the essential Baptist views and soon gathered followers around himself. He baptized Ezekiel Holliman, who then baptized Williams. Williams soon baptized ten others, and this small group organized themselves into a church. Apparently John Clarke came at about the same time from New Hampshire to Newport, and with no connection with the labors of Williams also organized a Baptist congregation.

The numerous divisions that now exist in the large Baptist family of denominations began to appear early. A Seventh-day Baptist body was begun in Newport, R.I., in 1671. Various disagreements occurred over the Calvanistic view of atonement. A colored Baptist Church was organized in 1788. In the Appalachian Mountains and other parts of the South came new Baptist movements, some holding to a stern Calvinism.

When missionary work was begun, many of the local groups opposed, not missions as such, but the organization necessary to carry on missions. The term "Primitive" came into use to designate those opposed to missionary organizations, and the popular word "Missionary Baptists" was used to name those in favor of missions. There was never a definite denominational organization named "Missionary," but several denominations put "Primitive" into their names.

Bodies other than Baptists hold certain Baptist views, particularly on baptism by immersion, the congregational form of government, and no official statement of creed. These include the Disciples of Christ, Churches of Christ, and various churches with Brethren in their official names. Many other bodies permit baptism by immersion as an alternate form. The Eastern Orthodox also practice baptism by immersion but do not limit it to persons of mature years.

Prior to the Civil War, in 1845, associations of Baptists in the Southern states formed the Southern Baptist Convention, now the largest denomination of Baptists with over 8,000,000 members. Today, many members and local churches of the Southern Baptists' Convention are in the Western states as well as in the South. The organization took place after disagreements with Baptists of the North over the issue of slavery. A missionary board with headquarters in Boston had taken a position that it would not be "a party to any arrangement which would imply approbation of slavery." About 300 churches in Southern states then set up their own organization for missionary work.

National organization proceeded slowly among churches committed to local control. The Northern Baptist Convention was not organized until 1907. It was renamed the American Baptist Convention in 1950.

Principal Beliefs and Doctrines. The doctrinal requirements of a member of the Baptist churches are at a minimum. Although various gatherings have formulated "confessions of faith," these are not binding on local churches or their members. Baptists have campaigned for freedom of conscience in religion and worship and have thus favored policies opposed to regimentation of thought among their members.

Baptists recognize two sacraments, baptism and the Lord's supper. Baptists in general believe in the validity and inspiration of the Scriptures, the Lordship of Christ, the immortality of the soul, the brotherhood of man, the future life, the need of redemption from sin, and the ultimate triumph of the Kingdom of God.

Forms of Worship. Baptists are "congregational" in form of worship. Thus the denomination prescribes no form or order of worship. In most churches the worship consists of hymns, prayer, Scripture reading, sermon, and offering, the order determined by the local church itself. In exceptional cases, the form of worship becomes more organized and approaches the liturgical.

Forms of Organization. As is clear from historical accounts, the form of organization of each Baptist body is strictly congregational, with the local church in full control of its own life and work. However, district, state, and national conventions are formed for carrying on and encouraging common interests and activities; and national boards administer programs in home and foreign missions, Christian education, etc.

BRETHREN CHURCHES. The term Brethren occurs in the name of several families of denominations. They are usually classified in three distinct groups.

1. BRETHREN, GERMAN BAPTIST. Of these there are five denominations, the largest being the Church of the Brethren, Elgin, Illinois, with 195,000 members. They evolved out of German pietism, which at the close of the seventeenth century was one of the influential movements for emphasizing the inner life of the Christian above creed or ritual or form or ceremony. This was a movement directed in part against an alleged barrenness and formalism of the Protestantism of the day. Among the leaders were Philip Jacob Spener and August Herman Francke, who conducted a mission and a school at Halle. They left a lasting testimony in the Church of the Brethren. They had no association with Mennonites or Friends who had similar purposes.

Congregations were organized in the Palatinate and other parts of Germany, and in Switzerland. From one of these, Crefeld, came the first Brethren to America, led by Peter Becker, who settled in Germantown, Pa., in 1719. History does not record what happened to the communities that remained in Europe. There are no members of the Church of Brethren in Europe today.

The Brethren of colonial days were popularly called Dunkers. The church is in general terms regarded as orthodox trinitarian. Baptism is by immersion. Plain attire is recommended. Nonresistance is taught. The members generally are conscientious objectors to military service. The ideal is to copy the life of the primitive Christians. Extensive relief work for needy persons abroad is carried on. Worship is informal, consisting of hymns, prayer, and preaching. The form of church government is closer to Presbyterian than any other. There have been a number of separations from this body. (CRB)

The five denominations of this group report about 240,-000 members in the U.S.A. (YBAC)

2. PLYMOUTH BRETHREN. Of these there are eight branches in the U.S.A. with about 25,000 members. The group also is organized in England. They consider the various denominations as unscriptural and do not engage in fellowship with other bodies. The different branches are in general accord. They accept the general evangelical doctrines of the Trinity, the absolute Deity of Christ, atonement by His sacrificial death, the verbal inspiration of the Scriptures. They meet in halls and private houses and do not have a professional ministry. (CRB)

3. RIVER BRETHREN. Of these there are three bodies with a total of 7,500 members in the United States. River Brethren is a popular term, having come from a "Brotherhood Down the River," Lancaster County, Pennsylvania, or from their custom of baptizing in a river. They arose out of groups advocating immersion and nonresistance. (CRB)

BUDDHISM. Buddhism is the religion founded by the Buddha in India in the sixth century, B.C. It has over 350,000,000 adherents in nine nations. The whole country of China is dotted with Buddhist temples, many of great beauty. Buddhists in large numbers are also found in Ceylon, Burma, Thailand, Indo-China, Korea, Japan, and in sections of the Soviet Union. In China many Buddhists are also Confucianists. In Japan, many Shintoists are also Buddhists.

Historical Notes. The young man Buddha, born Prince Siddharta c. 568, B.C., led a reform movement in protest against the formalism of the Hinduism in India of his day. Although the Buddha founded his religion in India, the number of his followers in that country is small, perhaps only 100,000 in a land of vast population.

The Buddha, the Enlightened One, led the princely sheltered life prescribed for him. But the young prince could ride forth in his realm, and thus he saw sights that made deep impressions on him. He saw people ill, old, and suffering, and religious people unconcerned. One day he resolved to consider the meaning of what he saw and the ways whereby men should live. He soon renounced his royal rights and set out to find the Truth that would save man. He wandered about for seven years, visiting with many people, including holy men and teachers. Sometimes their answers to his questions left him perplexed. But he became widely known as a holy man.

Living an ascetic life, highly disciplined, he practiced meditation. Remove ignorance, remove selfishness, remove the thirst for things, he reasoned. Blessed becomes he who understands the good Law. Blessed is he who overcomes sin and is free from passion. The highest blessedness comes to him who conquers vanity and selfishness. He may become blessed, the holy, the perfect.

Soon he was recognized as the one wise, the one enlightened. Tradition has it that he once lingered under a tree seven times seven days, becoming aware of his emancipation. Those who passed by recognized him as a man of peace and majesty. To whom should he preach and teach? He began with five former ascetic companions near Benares. The Buddha taught them the way to immortality, to Nirvana. It is reported that men and animals were affected by him when he spoke.

Principal Beliefs and Teachings. He urged men to cleanse their minds: to avoid extremes of austerity and of sensuality. He taught the wheel of the Excellent Law, which consisted of a hub of truth, a tire of wisdom, and spokes of pure conduct.

He set forth four noble truths:

1. The truth of suffering.
2. The cause of suffering.
3. The cessation of suffering.
4. The means of overcoming suffering.

The methods are an eight-fold path, often called "the middle way":

1. Right views.
2. Right aspirations.
3. Right speech.
4. Right conduct.
5. Right livelihood.
6. Right endeavor.
7. Right mindfulness.
8. Right meditation.

These are simply the foundations, the cornerstones, of Buddhism. The ultimate aim has been called the transformation of the personality. The path is a method of habit formation.

Buddha did not teach a personal deity. He emphasized

"Kharma" as the moral law of the universe. He also had no interest in rituals and originally did not think of a priesthood. Today, Buddhists refer to Buddha as the great example, but every person is called upon to seek his own enlightenment. Selflessness and the seeking of peace on earth are taught.

Originating 500 years before Christ many of the accounts of Buddha are much the same in detail as those about Christ. In Buddhist literature there is a marriage feast, a prodigal son, the Buddha dining with sinners, a rich young man seeking deliverance, a woman at the well. Buddha taught: "Overcome evil with good. . . . Purify your hearts. . . . Self is death, truth is life." There is a story of the mustard seed in Buddhist literature.

Nirvana as taught by the Buddhists means a state of no flame of selfish desire—no passion. It is akin to teachings of other religions to deny self and find true life. It does not mean to attain to a state of indifference, or of unconsciousness. It signifies a state of attaining to an expansion of personality—a larger consciousness.

Divisions. After the death of the leader came division. The simple abodes of the Buddha and his immediate followers were succeeded by monasteries, shrines, and temples. The simple teachings of the master teacher became subjects of speculation. Sects developed. Two great groups emerged:

The Mahayana, or Greater Vehicle, or Northern Buddhism. This group developed its own scripture, including the Lotus Gospel. It also produced an elaborate theology with the Buddha regarded as a divine savior.

The Hinayana, or Lesser Vehicle, or Southern Buddhism, which regards Buddha as not a supernatural being. Theology is less elaborate.

Era of Expansion. About 200 years after Buddha died there came an era of missionary endeavor largely as a result of the conversion of an emperor, Asoka. He came to rule in 272 B.C. and soon governed a large area. He took his religion seriously and his reign was marked by many constructive practices. He endowed numerous Buddhist temples, built hospitals, promoted education, taught and exemplified moral standards. He sent missionaries to other nations. In Ceylon, Burma, Cambodia, and Siam, Hinayana Buddhism, strongly monastic, became well established. Mahayana Buddhism moved to the north, going into China prior to the Christian era. From China it went to Korea and to Japan. But by the sixth century, A.D., it was declining in India, and by the thirteenth it had almost disappeared. As before noted, there are relatively few Buddhists in India but the Buddha is revered as a great man by the Indian people. Buddhism was vigorously opposed in India by the Hindus and still more effectively by invading Moslems.

Great Council. The Sixth Great Council of Buddhism was convened in Rangoon, Burma, 1954-56, for the purpose of re-examining the teachings of the religion. Laymen and monks by thousands took part. The government of Burma provided the buildings, and the Parliament of that nation took the initiative in calling the council. The members of the Parliament called for consideration of new measures for the spiritual and moral well-being of man.

CHINESE SAGES—CONFUCIUS AND LAO-TZU. The Chinese philosophers Confucius and Lao-tzu both lived at the time of Buddha.

Confucius was an educator and statesman, a philosopher and a practical man who has been called the symbol and model of all things Chinese. For almost 2,500 years many Chinese people have recorded their debt to this man and have acknowledged him as the most powerful single force in their ancient culture.

Confucianism is often called philosophy rather than religion, but many people have certainly regarded it as a religion. In China what we term Confucianism is called Ju Chaio, the teachings of the scholar. These teachings embrace those of Confucius and other tradition that has been developed over the centuries.

Confucius, born 551 B.C. in Shantung, was not the originator of this body of teaching. He studied the past and simply made formulations of the religion of the people of the past. His own references to religion are usually indirect and not frequent.

Confucius was a government employee when a young man. At age twenty-two he began to teach and soon had many students as followers. Out of his talks to these students, sometimes numbering several thousand, came the *Classics* that he edited.

Shortly after reaching the age of fifty, Confucius became administrator of justice in the state of Lu. His capacities were great and the practical effects remarkable. So marked were the results that the state was envied by a neighboring ruler, who influenced the Prince of Lu against Confucius. Confucius resigned and went from state to state seeking an employer, in vain. He returned to his native place and edited the compilations: *The Book of History, The Book of Poetry, The Book of Changes,* and *The Book of Rites*. His closing years were sad. In all the land there was not one monarch who would make him a minister.

After his death came disciples to bring together his own sayings: *The Confucian Analects*. They also brought out other works based upon Confucian teachings: *The Great Learning* and *The Doctrine of the Mean*. Two centuries later Mencius wrote somewhat popular versions of Confucius' sayings: *The Works of Mencius*.

Although writing little about the gods, Confucius became among many of the people the object of worship. Early in the twentieth century, his followers gave him a rank equal to heaven and earth. His complete veneration had been achieved, and he was praised in hundreds of temples. But with the coming of the Republican era, the edifices fell into poor repair, and Confucius was formally revered only by old teachers.

The number of Confucianists today can hardly be estimated. There may be 300,000,000, but many Confucianists are also Buddhists or Taoists.

For a brief period, under Japanese occupation of parts of China, the teachings of Confucius were ordered restored in the schools. Under the present Communist regime the *Classics* is reported to have been suppressed. To what extent the ethical teachings of Confucius would live on among the people, without formal teaching, cannot be stated. The main teachings are:

The nature of man is good.
Man possesses free will to make choices.
Virtue brings its own reward—one does not refrain from evil because of fear of punishment.
"What you do not want others to do unto you, do not do unto them."

Confucius urged filial piety. He sought the moral cultivation of "the princely man" as the cornerstone of "the good society."

Among the steps in moral cultivation are:

Knowledge of the final objective.
Rectification of the heart.
Sincerity of purpose.

Lao-tzu, sometimes spelled Lao-tze, (sixth century, B.C.) known as the founder of Taoism in China, expounded doctrines much at variance with those of Confucius. The number of present-day followers is not determinable, although Taoist priests function in a number of communities. It is believed to be a religion of the uneducated. There may be 50,000,000 adherents. Observers appear to agree that present-day organization and practice have little resemblance to the beautiful words and ideas of the founder. Practical acts of service are recommended by the teachers, but priests are reported to be of a low order.

Lao-tzu wrote in language of power and grace. "A constant giver is the man who loves." "We must be able to be at peace in order to be active in love." "All beings will be transformed from within themselves."

He advocated the practice of daily periods of silence. He taught that men should return good for evil. He taught unity, selflessness, the endlessness of man's real life, the high value of the inner life versus outer possessions.

He was continually interpreting the Tao, the Way. This was something mysterious. There is no word, no combination of words, to describe it. He called it "great" in endeavoring to describe it. The law of the Tao is its own spontaneity. It is the mother of the universe but its name is not known to the teacher. Possibly he came in his writing closer to certain of the teachings of Jesus in the

Sermon on the Mount than any other religious teacher.

CHRISTIANITY. The term Christian was first used by the people of the important city of Antioch, Syria, to designate the followers of Jesus Christ. It is derived from the Greek word, Christos (Christ), for the Messiah, or anointed one. As an adjective derived from a personal name, the ending (ian) is Latin in origin. The adjective may have been originally used without intent to compliment. But no matter what its precise origin, it was a term soon used by the disciples of Jesus, and in portions of the New Testament. Among Biblical references are *Acts* 11: 26; 26:28.

Adherents of Christianity are found in three great branches, or divisions: Roman Catholic, Eastern Orthodox, and Protestant, all of which are described herein. The total Christian constituency is estimated to number some 895,000,000 persons, or about one-third of the world's population.

Christianity may be thought of in terms of the scope of its organizations; systems of thought and teaching; as a quality of life in imitation of the life of Jesus Christ, the founder. In the articles on various branches, references are made to all three.

The main sources of the life of Jesus are the four Gospels, which are brief biographies, recognized as works of art because of beauty of language in certain translations. Probably the four Gospels of Matthew, Mark, Luke, and John are those that survived among other writings in existence in the early years of the Christian era.

Other important early documents of which there are records are the Epistles of Paul. These, it is believed, were in some way preserved by churches in the cities to which they were sent. They were probably read to the people along with the Old Testament scriptures. The present New Testament took form in the fourth century. The writings of the Church Fathers also constitute a large literature. These throw light on the nature of early Christian communities.

Jesus Christ was born in Bethlehem of Judea, about 6 B.C. An error in the making of the calendar centuries ago accounts for this date, because time has been reckoned from His birth. The lack of data in the Gospels also makes it impossible to present a precise date. The Gospels of Matthew and Luke record that Jesus was born of the Virgin Mary, but the two other Gospels do not mention His virgin birth or give any details of His youth. At age twelve He came to public notice, but it was not until He was thirty that His public ministry began. He was baptized by John and then underwent great experiences and began His public teaching.

He is designated the Messiah, the anointed one, in the New Testament. But His own acceptance and His own language were such that He excluded from the concept the main elements of the popular ideal—that of the hero who would rescue the Jewish people from their oppressors. His own disciples undoubtedly thought of two main ideas: 1) They saw Jesus as the spiritual Messiah, the servant of Jehovah who would suffer for and teach the people; 2) they looked forward to His second coming in power and glory to rule over the nations.

The first disciples whom Christ called to Himself were fishermen. Others of the twelve were artisans, or craftsmen; one was a tax gatherer, not a popular figure.

Jesus had remarkable powers of healing. He taught of

God as the Father of all men. He spoke in simple language, and many of His stories, parables, are vivid in their simplicity and unique in the power of their teaching. He spoke of a Kingdom to come, and also as one that was already within men. He had compassion for the unfortunate and the handicapped.

He told people to love their enemies and to resist evil. He spoke with authority and His language of rebuke to insincerity was not mild. People flocked to hear Him, and the number of His opponents also increased.

During a Passover season (a Jewish spring festival), He was tried on the charge of blasphemy and sentenced to death by the Roman magistrate, Pilate. He was crucified on a cross between two thieves. On the third day following, His disciples reported the tomb empty, and soon some of His disciples stated that they had seen Him. Probably most Christians have been convinced that there was a resurrection of the body. Others believe there was a resurrection of the spirit.

His disciples preached, in confident hope, a Christ who was alive. They associated in little bands. The authoritative voice of the church that was created by Jesus' followers declared him to be God and Saviour, who promised salvation to mankind. Thus, in Christianity, the name of God is a Trinity, who exists in three persons: Father, Son and Holy Spirit. This doctrine was accepted early in the Christian era and was discussed and amplified in the great ecumenical, or universal, councils. Trinitarianism is the norm in Christian circles; the minority rejecting the concept are called Unitarian. The generally accepted statement of the doctrine is that the three persons are equal, eternal, and indivisible. But in most theologies the teaching is a mystery that cannot be understood fully by man. It is regarded as a truth that comes through revelation.

Important Eras of Christianity

1. The Apostolic Age, to about 45 A.D. The beginning of the Christian Church is usually thought of as the meeting in the upper room at Jerusalem on the Day of Pentecost, after the ascension of Jesus into heaven. The first Christians were Jews who undoubtedly continued to worship in the Jewish Temple. But early Christians met in houses and broke bread.

2. The Era of St. Paul. The Pharisee, Paul of Tarsus, converted in 35 A.D., was the genius who united Hebrew, Greek, and Roman ideas and became the Apostle to the Gentiles. He widened the scope of the religion and took it to distant shores. He set out on his first missionary journey in 45 A.D. He died in 67 A.D

3. The spread of the church among gentiles, 67 to 1054. This era was marked by the acceptance of Christianity by the Emperor Constantine (272-327) in Rome. He became a patron of the new religion and gave it recognition as one of the religions of the Empire.

4. The Division into East and West, in 1054. The Eastern Church came under the influence of the Emperor who was ruler in Constantinople. In the West, under the Church in Rome, the great event was probably the mass conversion of the German peoples. Christianity spread to the British Isles and northern Europe.

5. The Reformation. Martin Luther (1483-1536), an Augustinian monk in Germany, became in 1517 the effective leader of a series of reform movements, although there were other—less extensive—developments before

his day. (See Lutheran churches.) The Western Church became divided, and the era of modern denominations began. (See the articles on Eastern Orthodox, Roman Catholicism, Protestantism and its denominations.)

The Bible. This is the name given by Christians to their Scriptures. It consists of Old Testament, New Testament, and Apocrypha. Various translations are in use. The Old Testament is the older part, of Jewish authorship. The Jews established their recognized text about 100 A.D. The New Testament in its present form was agreed upon in the fourth century. All the major Christian churches use the same New Testament, consisting of twenty-seven books: four biographies of Jesus, named Gospels; a historical account of early activities of Christians, the Acts of the Apostles; twenty-one letters called Epistles; and, finally, the Apocalypse or Revelation. The books of the New Testament contain only a portion of early Christian literature. The Apocrypha refers to a group of books regarded by Christians as of doubtful use or authority. When it appears in Bibles, the Apocrypha is printed between the Old and New Testaments.

During recent years numerous translations of the Bible have been made because of discoveries that led to new knowledge of sources. Among these are the Confraternity translations being made by Roman Catholic scholars in the U.S.A., the printing of which was begun with the New Testament in 1941; and the Revised Standard Version by Protestant scholars in the U.S.A., completed in 1952. A version in wide use is the King James, or authorized version, 1611. The beautiful English used in this translation has had a marked influence on English letters. The Douay version was brought out by Roman Catholic scholars in 1610.

CHRISTIAN SCIENCE. Christian Science is the religion of the Church of Christ, Scientist, founded by Mary Baker Eddy at Boston, Massachusetts, in 1879. Its interpretation of the Bible teachings reduces them to a science whose adoption and application, it is claimed, heals the body by mental or spiritual regeneration. It is one of the relatively few religious bodies to originate in the U.S.A. The Church of Christ, Scientist, now has a regulation forbidding the numbering of the people and the reporting of such statistics for publication. In 1936, the federal Census of Religious Bodies recorded 268,915 members in 2,113 local churches and members in The Mother Church not affiliated with any local church or society. The churches are found in most cities of the U.S.A. and in many large cities throughout the world. There are now more than 3,100 local units throughout the world. (YBAC)

Historical Notes. Mrs. Eddy began to teach this religion at Lynn, Mass., in 1866. She first issued her textbook, *Science and Health, with Key to the Scriptures* in 1875.

For years prior to 1866, Mrs. Eddy studied religion and mental causes and effects. She became inclined to attribute causation to God and to regard Him as Divine Mind. She stated that she had recovered almost instantly in 1866 from a severe injury after reading in the Gospel of Matthew an account of a healing. The origin of the religion followed this incident.

Mrs. Eddy taught and wrote and in due course decided that a church became a necessity to facilitate cooperation among Christian Scientists. Thus she organized the Church of Christ, Scientist, in order "to commemorate the word and works of our Master," and "to reinstate primitive Christianity and its lost element of healing."

Mrs. Eddy made the final revision of her book, *Science and Health*, in 1907. She is also the author of other works found in many Christian Science reading rooms. The Church of Christ, Scientist, publishes much other literature, including periodicals, available in these rooms.

Principal Beliefs and Doctrines. Christian Science is a religious teaching and practice based on the words of Jesus Christ. As further defined by Mrs. Eddy, the religion is a "divine metaphysics"; "a scientific system of divine healing"; "the law of God, the law of Good, interpreting and demonstrating the divine principle and rule of universal harmony." God is "All-in-all." He is the "Divine Principle of all that really is." Jesus Christ is the "Way-shower." His chief work is the atonement, regarded as "exemplification of man's unity with God, whereby man reflects divine Truth, Life, Love." (CRB)

The practice of Christian Science is not limited to the healing of the sick—its adherents state that their religion may be applied to practically every human need. The practice of Christian Science is also not confined to the mental—it is truly mental only if it is truly spiritual.

The church has a number of trained practitioners and readers. The practitioner and reader who wishes co aid another person must know that his power comes from the Divine Mind. He must recognize: "I can of mine own self do nothing." (*John* V:30)

Form of Worship. The principal part of the Sunday services is the lesson-sermon, which is prepared by a committee connected with the Mother Church. It is read, as prepared, by two readers who stand before the congregation and read alternately; the first reader reads from Mrs. Eddy's book, *Science and Health*, and the second reader reads from the Bible. A Wednesday evening testimony meeting is held, conducted by the first reader, at which are given the public testimonies of those who have been healed and reformed by Christian Science. There are also public lectures.

Form of Organization. The local branch churches have the right of self-government but must carry out the prescribed form of worship. The Mother Church in Boston is controlled by a Board of Directors, which is also the governing body of the denomination.

Membership in this denomination is open to persons twelve years of age and over, who are not members of another denomination, who are of Christian character, and who believe in and declare that they understand Christian Science.

CHURCHES OF CHRIST. The Churches of Christ and the Disciples of Christ (which see) have a common origin in movements in the United States in the early part of the nineteenth century when a number of leaders made pleas for a return to the Bible alone, with no human addition in the form of creeds and formulas. Among these leaders were Thomas Campbell, who had been a minister of the Secession Branch of the Presbyterian Church in Ireland, and his son, Alexander Campbell, who formed a Christian Association at Washington, Pennsylvania, in 1809. This association issued a declaration of the position summarized above.

Local churches soon sprang up, holding up the primitive church as example. Controversies came over the use of instrumental music, some churches deciding against organs. Thus came parties called "conservatives" and "progressives." About the year 1900, the conservatives came to be known as the Churches of Christ, and the progressives as the Disciples of Christ.

In doctrine and policy the two groups are in general accord. Each local group is independent. The Churches of Christ have no general organization of the local churches. Baptism is by immersion. The Lord's supper is held as a memorial service each Lord's Day. (CRB)

The Churches of Christ have established churches abroad in Italy, Africa, Mexico, Latin America and the Far East. They report 1,600,000 members in the United States (YBAC), with no estimates available for other nations. There is no general organization or headquarters. A periodical, *The Gospel Advocate,* is published at Nashville, Tennessee.

CHURCH OF CHRIST, SCIENTIST, *see Christian Science*

CHURCHES OF GOD. There are many denominations with the name of Church of God or with these words as part of the title. One way of avoiding a degree of confusion has been to add the address of the headquarters whenever the name is printed. Most of the denominations are described in CRB and YBAC.

These bodies emphasize the Scriptures as the authority for doctrine. They are trinitarian. They carry on intense evangelistic programs.

One body observing the seventh day as the Sabbath, Church of God, Salem, W.Va., reports tracing its origin to settlers from England who in Newport, R.I. organized one of these churches in 1664. It has about 2,000 members. (YBAC)

One of the larger bodies is at Anderson, Ind., with over 115,000 members. This body is the result of a movement within another Church of God (Winebrenner), in 1880, when D. S. Warner and others felt that the church was coming to be too restricted by human organization. They wished to have a church more directly under the rule of God. The movement was powerful through evangelism and spread particularly in the Middle West.

The Church of God, Anderson, Ind., is orthodox and evangelical. Adherents hold to the divine inspiration of the Scriptures; they believe in the Holy Trinity and in the personal second coming of Christ. They practice baptism by immersion and the Lord's Supper. They believe that the church is the body of Christ, made up of all Christians, but that denominations and sects are a hindrance to the expression of unity and are unscriptural. They believe that God is working to restore the New Testament ideal of his church.

Membership in this Anderson, Ind., Church of God is on an informal basis. It is reported that local churches generally keep no membership lists. Ministers are ordained by other ministers. In general, this body emphasizes spiritual experience rather than creedal agreement.

Another large body is the Assemblies of God, Springfield, Mo., with a membership of over 425,000. This body resulted from wide evangelistic and missionary work by independent pastors in the years 1906-1914. A desire for fellowship led to the formation of an organization in Arkansas in 1914.

The doctrine of the Assemblies of God emphasizes the inspiration of the Scriptures; sanctification as a goal for all believers; divine healing; the imminent coming of Jesus Christ to judge the world; everlasting punishment for the wicked; a new heaven and a new earth for true believers.

Worship in the local church is informal, stressing evangelistic preaching, along with prayer and hymns. In form of government, the Assemblies of God is a combination of the Congregational and Presbyterian systems. In addition to evangelism, the denomination promotes foreign and home missions and maintains schools for training its ministers.

In the U.S. there are eight denominations of Churches of God with 380,000 members. (YBAC) In Great Britain there are about 450 places of worship with number of members not reported. (WCH) No Canadian figures are available.

CONFUCIANISM, *see Chinese Sages*

CONGREGATIONAL CHRISTIAN CHURCHES. Congregationalism is an outgrowth of separatist sentiment and movements in England. After the Reformation came a school of thought holding that the whole system of an established church in England was an anti-Christian manifestation and could not be reformed, and that the only course for a Christian was to separate himself from it.

The Congregational Christian Churches report 1,300,-000 members in the United States. (YBAC) In Great Britain there are over 450,000 Congregationalists. Throughout the world there are probably about 2,000,000 adult members. (WCH) In Canada, the Congregationalists merged with other bodies to form the United Church of Canada in 1925. That church reports 875,000 members.

Historical Notes. In 1604, Separatism became organized as Congregationalism in a little congregation already organized in Scrooby, England. The pastor, John Robinson, had been in touch with Robert Browne, a Separatist pastor, who emigrated to Holland in 1581. From there he issued pamphlets with attacks on the ecclesiastical system of England. At least five men who distributed these pamphlets in England paid for their sentiments with their lives. Exile also became necessary for John Robinson, who went to Holland. In Leyden he encouraged a group of Separatists to emigrate to America, and from there went the Pilgrims. In Plymouth, Massachusetts, in 1620 the first Congregational Church of America was established. Robinson remained in Leyden. After periods of great difficulty, the church of the Puritans of Massachusetts Bay and that of the Pilgrims of Plymouth were united into American Congregationalism. By 1640 there were thirty-one churches in New England of the Congregational type. By 1648 there was an association of such churches.

Congregationalism spread westward with the population. It engaged in large home and foreign missions, education among the Negroes, and encouraged the formation of numerous colleges. Out of it came American Unitarianism (which see).

In 1924 the Evangelical Protestant Church of North America voted to become Congregational; and in 1931 the Christian Church, general convention, united with the Congregationalist to form the Congregational Christian Churches (headquarters in New York).

Principal Beliefs and Doctrines. Each local church has the right to formulate its own statement of doctrines. The General Council of the Congregational Christian Churches adopted a "platform," which has had general acceptance but is not binding upon the local church.

"We believe in God the Father, infinite in wisdom, goodness, and love; and in Jesus Christ, His Son, our Lord and Savior, who for us and our salvation lived and died and rose again and liveth evermore; and in the Holy Spirit, who taketh of the things of Christ and revealeth them to us, renewing, comforting, and inspiring the souls of men. We are united in striving to know the will of God, as taught in the Holy Scriptures, and in our purpose to walk in the ways of the Lord, made known or to be made known to us. We hold it to be the mission of the Church of Christ to proclaim the Gospel to all mankind, exalting the worship of the true God, and laboring for the progress of knowledge, the promotion of justice, the reign of peace, and the realization of human brotherhood. . . ." (CRB).

Infant baptism is practiced, and the Lord's Supper is offered to all followers of Christ.

Form of Worship. This body leaves the form of worship to the local unit. In actual practice, the Sunday service consists of hymns, scripture reading, prayer, sermon, offering.

Form of Organization. The local church is the unit of organization, and every church member has an equal voice in its conduct. The church officers function solely to assure orderly worship and effective administration. There are state associations of the churches, and a General Council, but these have no authority over the local body.

Plans have been approved by this body to merge it, in 1957, with the Evangelical and Reformed Church, to form a new United Church of Christ, which other bodies are invited to join. (See article on church unions, in III, below).

COPTIC CHURCH, *see Eastern Orthodox Churches*

DISCIPLES OF CHRIST. The Disciples of Christ and the Churches of Christ (which see) trace their origin to an organization formed at Washington, Pa., in 1809, by the Rev. Thomas Campbell and his son, Alexander, named "The Christian Association."

There is a World Convention of Churches of Christ (Disciples), New York, which reports about 2,100,000 members throughout the world. Of these 1,890,000 are in the United States; 8,300 in Canada; 9,500 in Great Britain; 83,500 in Africa; 31,000 in Australia, and smaller numbers in each of twenty-five other nations.

Historical Note. This Christian Association issued a statement setting forth the essential unity of the Church of Christ, holding that there should be no schisms or uncharitable divisions, and that the Scripture should be the only basis of organization. Thomas Campbell had been a minister of the Secession Branch of the Presbyterian Church in Ireland.

Division among Christians was called "anti-Christian." The Campbells alleged that they did not wish to originate a new denomination. At first the publication of the statement elicited little response. The authors sought to associate themselves with Presbyterian and Baptist groups, but difficulties arose. In 1810, there was formed the "First Church of the Christian Association of Washington, meeting at Cross Roads and Brush Run, Washington County, Pa." Barton W. Stone, another Presbyterian clergyman, joined forces with Alexander Campbell in 1832.

The spread of the movement was rapid, especially in the Middle West. During the Civil War there was disorganization, and afterward came the formation of parties, e.g., those opposed to instrumental music, those opposed to missionary organization. After a period the churches generally grouped themselves into the conservatives, the Churches of Christ, while the progressives came under the term Disciples of Christ. Locally, the churches are generally called Christian Churches, in both groups.

Principle Beliefs and Doctrines. The Disciples accept the divine inspiration of the Holy Scriptures, the sufficiency of the Bible as the Revelation of God's will and as the rule of faith and life; the revelation of God in the threefold personality of Father, Son and Holy Spirit; the divine glory of Christ, His incarnation, doctrine, miracles, resurrection, ascension; the obligation of the divine ordinances of baptism and the Lord's Supper.

Form of Worship. The order of worship is in the control of the local congregation. It is the custom to celebrate the Lord's Supper as a memorial service each Lord's Day. The service consists of hymns, prayer, Scripture reading, sermon, and offering, as may be locally determined.

Form of Organization: The Disciples are congregational. There is in the U.S.A. an International Convention of Disciples of Christ, Indianapolis, composed of individual members of the local churches. Those attending have a personal rather than a representative status. The convention has no authority over the churches. Societies and boards carry on missions and educational programs.

DUNKERS, *see Brethren Churches*

EASTERN ORTHODOX CHURCHES. The Holy Eastern Orthodox Church considers itself to be the direct heir and true conserver of the Church of the first Christian era. It also claims the title "Catholic." Many of its churches assume they are "Catholic"; others have the term "Catholic" in their official titles. The Eastern Orthodox Church is in modern times popularly called "Greek Catholic" and was in early centuries called "Eastern Catholic." It has been called "the old church." It arose as the one holy Catholic and Apostolic Church of the Byzantine Empire.

There are twenty-one branches of the Orthodox in the United States, with 2,400,000 members. There can be no reliable figure of the number throughout the world, because of the difficulty of making an estimate for the Soviet Union. For the world as a whole, the number of Eastern Orthodox is estimated variously from 145,000,000 to 175,-000,000 persons. These are mainly in the Soviet Union, the nations bordering the Soviet on the West, and in nations of the Middle East.

Historical Notes: The foundations of the church in form and doctrine were established by the ecumenical councils. (The word ecumenical means world-wide.) These councils were convocations of the whole church and were generally accepted by the whole church. The Orthodox recognize seven of these councils beginning with the one in Nicea in the year 325 and ending with the seventh of the series, the second to meet in Nicea, in 787.

The Orthodox Church consists of a number or autonomous churches, the oldest of which are the four eastern patriarchs of Constantinople, Alexandria, Antioch, and Jerusalem. Two world wars have left their marks in the form of many alterations in the organizations of Orthodoxy, particularly in the nations bordering Russia, and also in the United States, as a result of the political changes which have affected those Orthodox churches which were emigrations from Russia.

These various churches, although independent of one another ecclesiastically, are nevertheless in essential agreement in form of worship and in doctrine.

Principal Beliefs and Doctrines. In doctrine, the Orthodox churches recognize Christ as the head of the church. The doctrine is founded on the Holy Scriptures, the traditions, and the decisions of the seven ecumenical councils. Thus the Scriptures are interpreted in accordance with the pronouncements of the ecumenical councils. One of the fundamental differences between the Orthodox churches and the Roman Catholic Church is that the Orthodox do not recognize the primacy of the Pope. Also, the Orthodox say the Nicene Creed to indicate their belief that the Holy Ghost proceeds from the Father alone, and do not say, as do Roman Catholics, "and from the Son."

The Orthodox honor Mary as the mother of God. They hold to the Catholic doctrine of the Virgin birth of Christ. They do not define as dogma the doctrine of the immaculate conception of the Virgin Mary. They do not hold to the doctrine of indulgences. They revere relics of the saints, pictures of holy objects, and the cross, but do not allow the use of carved images.

Form of Worship. The liturgy of the Church is always sung. Raised bread is used when the sacrifice is offered. Edifices are generally square and have a solid screen separating the sanctuary from the main body of the church. The sacraments are in general the same as those of the Catholic West, but are observed with a number of variations. Confession is less common than in the Roman Catholic Church, and the liturgy is usually not celebrated daily. Priests may be married.

The Orthodox offer the holy communion to all members after confession and absolution, except that children under seven receive the sacrament without confession. The Orthodox consider that both faith and works are necessary for justification. All persons who have been baptized and received the sacrament of Chrismation (confirmation), which follows baptism immediately, are communicants.

The service of the Orthodox churches is solemn, elaborate, and widely regarded as of great beauty.

Form of Organization. There are three orders of the ministry—deacons, priests, and bishops. The deacons assist in the work of the parish and in the service of the sacraments. Priests and deacons are of two orders, secular and monastic. Marriage is allowed to candidates for the diaconate and the priesthood, but is forbidden after ordination. Monastic orders are maintained, and usually bishops are chosen from members of a monastic order. The organization for the general government of the different churches varies in different countries. In general, there is a council at the head of which, as president, is a bishop elected by the ecclesiastical representatives of the people.

The Coptic Church is like the Eastern Orthodox churches except for the part of its dogma relating to the nature of Christ. The Copts hold to Monophysitism, a dogma declaring that Jesus Christ had not two natures, but one. (The Catholic teaching is that Jesus Christ is of two distinct natures, divine and human, and that these two are together in one person in hypostatic union.) The Copts are a small Christian minority in Egypt. Present-day Copts there are descended from the Egyptians who lived in that nation pior to the Muslim invasion. The Copts in

Egypt speak Arabic. In Egypt and other Middle-Eastern nations, there are reported about 10,000,000 adherents.

EPISCOPAL CHURCH, *see Anglicans*

EVANGELISTIC ASSOCIATIONS. Here may be grouped a number of associations of local churches whose main characteristic is conducting evangelistic work, and, in some instances, foreign missions. They are dominated by the concept of evangelism rather than by their doctrine or by their form of organization. Not one of these churches is large, only one reporting as many as 10,000 members. Eleven denominations within this group in the United States report 37,000 members. (YBAC)

The largest of these bodies are the Apostolic Christian Church of America, Morton, Ill., 7,700 members; the Christian Congregation, Augusta, Texas, 12,860 members; Missionary Church Association, Fort Wayne, Ind., 6,700 members; Pillar of Fire, Zarephath, N.J., 5,100 members.

FRIENDS. The Religious Society of Friends dates from the activities of George Fox in England in the middle of the seventeenth century.

There are about 180,000 Friends in the world, including 120,000 in the United States, 22,000 in Great Britain, 20,-000 in East Africa, and smaller numbers in a score of other nations. (Figures from Friends World Committee, American Section, Philadelphia.)

Historical Notes. Britain in the first half of the seventeenth century was in the midst of violent religious struggles and discussions. George Fox, born in 1624, was a serious youth who dwelt on the spiritual aspects of Christianity which he felt were being ignored in the midst of emphasis on creeds and formalism in religious bodies. Fox soon gathered around himself a group of preachers who emphasized "the inner light." Like many others, they seem at first not to have intended that they should form a new organization, but this was soon the result of their activities. These preachers went throughout Britain, to the continent of Europe, the West Indies, and North America.

One of the names they gave themselves was Friends of Truth, and after a time, Religious Society of Friends, the name now used. They often added, "commonly called Quakers." The word Quaker was first used as a term of derision. It was applied to Fox and his followers by an unfriendly justice, upon whom Fox called to "tremble at the word of God." The refusal of the Friends to participate in the established church resulted in severe persecution.

Friends came to Massachusetts in 1656, where they were put under arrest and sent back to Barbados, whence they had come. Friends continued to come and to encounter all sorts of restrictions, until in 1724 they were permitted peaceably to settle in Massachusetts. They encountered trying experiences in Virginia and Connecticut, but were welcomed in Rhode Island and seem to have had satisfactory experiences in New York, New Jersey, and Maryland. The main immigration, of course, was to Pennsylvania under the leadership of William Penn, who received land for a colony there in return for a debt due from the British Crown to his father, Admiral Penn.

Principal Beliefs and Doctrines. Friends do not have a formal creed. They emphasize the personal teaching of the Holy Spirit, "the Light Within." They advocate simple architecture and furnishings in their meeting houses. They do not emphasize outward ordinances. They have a most democratic form of conducting business. They teach peace and nonresistance, in accord with which most Friends do not consistently undertake military service or directly support wars.

Form of Worship. The largest group of Friends in the United States, Five Years Meetings, conducts programed services and employs ministers. Another group, General Conference, conducts worship without program. They appoint a time and place for the worship, and participation is left to the individual. By this method there are often long periods of silence which are considered important in the process of worship.

Organizations. Separations occurred among the Friends in the early part of the nineteenth century. One of the main divisions occurred through the activities of Elias Hicks in 1827 who led a so-called liberal movement. This was, in part, an aspect of the Unitarian-Trinitarian controversy of the time. The liberal group also adopted no formal creed but held that each person should have the right to determine for himself that which he thought to be true.

Since 1917, the various branches of Friends have carried on an increasing number of common activities, particularly through the American Friends Service Committee, Philadelphia.

ETHICAL CULTURE MOVEMENT. The Ethical Culture Movement was formally founded when Felix Adler organized the New York Society for Ethical Culture in 1876. Since then other societies have been formed in American cities, in Eastern Europe, and Japan. A federation of local societies has been organized, the American Ethical Union, New York, 1886. The local societies are completely autonomous. They also have made no formal expression of doctrine.

The leaders of the Ethical Culture Movement state that it is bound up with man's religious tradition and with the wisdom of philosophers. They revere the best in the traditional faiths and attempt to interpret ethical teachings in such a way as to develop man's spiritual life today. It is a purpose of the Ethical Movement to help men to become aware of the worth of human personality, of the unique value of every human being, of the interdependence of human life, and of the possibilities of creative relationships.

There are about 5,500 members in the United States. (YBAC)

The movement has established Ethical Culture schools for elementary and secondary education. They have encouraged experimental programs. These schools are open to persons regardless of their religious views or affiliations. (CRB)

HINDUISM. This is a term describing a religion among people mainly in India. (The Hindus, however, in their language of Sanskrit have no precise word for religion. The corresponding word is one meaning such ideas as right, duty, good works.) There are about 300,000,000 Hindus. Most are in India; some 200,000 in South Africa; some 135,000 in Trinidad; a few thousands in Ceylon, Burma, and Malaya.

Historical Notes. Unlike many other religions, the origins of Hinduism cannot be traced to the life or teaching of any one person. Its origins are found in the various natural religions of the ancient people of India who had a very old civilization. Among the oldest scriptures of the world are the *Rig-Veda,* containing 1,200 hymns addressed to the various gods—of fire, of sunlight, of wind, etc.

Later came the *Upanishads,* which are about a universal spirit and a creative principle. They thus deal with the reality behind nature and man's relation to it. They are exalted writings expressing moral insights.

In the course of the centuries, a number of teachers and prophets appeared, and their writings and admonitions have been heeded. They are also revered and regarded as incarnations of divinity. Thus among the people generally there are many gods, some coming from the ancient days. But among people more interested in intellectual systems there have evolved important groups or sects or schools of thought, and also notable contributions to the philosophy of religion.

Principal Beliefs and Doctrines. One of these is Brahmanism, a religion with a triune deity: Brahma, the source and the giver of life; Vishnu, the preserver; and Siva, the destroyer.

Just as there are varied—and extreme—elements which are the result of long centuries of experience, so there are common ideas and principles:

1. A belief in Kharma, which literally means action, also called the law of the deed.

2. A belief in the transmigration of souls, holding that the individual has lived many lives before this one and will live many more until the time of final liberation.

3. An emphasis on the ascetic life.

4. Regard for the practice of the Kharma, noted above
—law, custom, etc.

5. Observance of the caste system (against which, however, there have been strong popular movements recently).

The reverence of the orthodox Hindu for all of life is
consistent and often the subject of comment. The orthodox Hindu will not eat a fertile egg, will not kill a fly, and
will not slay a cow. The maintenance of large numbers of
aged cows is often thought to deter people from raising
their standards of life in the villages. But the cows are
also defended as economic assets in the village economy:
the cow is a beast of burden who pulls a plow; it supplies
milk; it also supplies dung which is used for fuel as well
as fertilizer.

Yoga is a method of the Hindus. It is an attitude to
attain union with God, a method of freeing and unfolding
the personality and uniting the spirit of man with the
supreme creative spirit of the universe. By exercising
thought and nerve control over many years, many extraor-
dinary powers are achieved. They are years of silent
devotion, simplicity of personal habits, and of the single
heart. Then the soul may attain illumination.

There are about sixty sects or denominations in Hinduism, worshiping some type of personal deity. In the
Bhagavad-Gita, possibly the most widely used of the
Hindu scriptures, Krishna becomes the supreme God.
(Krishna is one of the numerous incarnations of Vishnu,
noted above, "the preserver.") There is wide reverence
for Krishna, the beautiful child. In the *Gita,* Krishna is
regarded as the savior of the world, and in these writings
are also found deep ethical insights.

Ideas of salvation have been developing in Hinduism.

The reverence for Krishna implies salvation by a relation of faith in and loyalty to the great personality and incarnation. This idea is added to the earlier ideas of salvation by works or good deeds, and salvation by knowledge, the last having been emphasized by the philosophers of Hinduism.

The Caste System. The code calling for four castes came down from early eras and has had religious sanction. It outlined special duties of each caste. It is also believed that the rigidities that developed were never taught by the originators. The four castes are:

1. Brahmans, who are to be the priests and sages, teaching the results of their search for truth to the people generally.

2. Kshatriyas, those who govern and protect, and through their administration of practical affairs advance the public interest—not their own.

3. Vaisyas, those with productive crafts and trades, who are to produce and distribute the world's goods fairly and justly.

4. Sudras, the laborers, whose duty is to serve and also to learn by observation of others in society.

Relations between castes have been regulated. For example, intermarriage has been prohibited. In extreme cases, as in Southern India where most rigidity prevailed, laborers might not walk the same streets as the Brahmans.

There are students of Hinduism who say that the caste system once made for a healthy society, when all four types were accorded equal respect. But exclusiveness developed, as elsewhere in the world, and the Sudras became "outcasts" and "untouchables."

Mohandas Gandhi, perhaps the best known Hindu of recent times, led strong movements for reform of the abuses and for abolition of the discriminations against the untouchables.

Many Hindu leaders are believed to be opposed to absolute abolition of the caste system. They would try to recover some of the original meaning of the system with its mutual respect. They would like to preserve the special duties of a vocation, with codes similar to those of the guilds or professions.

In India, untouchability is now illegal, according to the constitution, but public custom and practice do not always conform. It is generally agreed that it will take time to achieve enforcement. When there is better observance, there will be better enforcement.

Observers notice in India a distinct interpretation of "Kharma" as implying service to others. This has given stimulus to interest in social reform.

Form of Worship. Hinduism is distinguished for numerous temples and shrines, found in every village. There are also sacred cities, of which Benares is probably best known. Many people make pilgrimages to Benares, where they bathe in the Ganges River and also worship in the numerous temples and shrines.

The Hindus, along with others, think that man in his worship needs concrete forms around which to center his thoughts and aspirations. Thus numerous images are found in the temples. In Hinduism these images are the means whereby large numbers of persons worship a personal god. Like masses of people in other nations, the people of India who are Hindus worship God in a human form, a person in whom is incarnated perfect qualities.

Form of Organization. Hinduism maintains no organized ecclesiastical hierarchy. The temples are often erected and maintained by people of means in the community. The priests in the temples draw their living from the gifts of these persons and from the offerings of those who worship. The paid priests of the temples are, however, but one type of special religious leadership. There are also numerous *sannyasins*, or monks, who are devout men and regarded as persons with religious insights. They include men of great learning and the utmost dedication. These holy men have imitators who wander around and live as beggars. The story is told that an English visitor once complained to the noted literary figure, Rabindranath Tagore, that there were 9,000,000 monks wandering about India begging from the populace. Tagore is reported to have replied that there were probably that many, and it would be worth while to maintain that many since there were nine saints among them. He also inquired whether there were nine saints in England.

Reform Movements. There have been great reform movements within Hinduism. One of the most extensive is Buddhism, which arose in India, but now has few followers there, and which is considered separately. Others are Jainism, which see; and Sikhism, which see. In more recent years the impact of Western contacts is believed to have been one of the forces making for other marked reform movements. Two of these are:

BRAHMA AAMAJ, begun by Ram Mohan Ray, in 1828. He organized a society, gave the people an opportunity to take part in worship (unlike the temple worship), and opposed aspects of the caste system. His successors have advocated the formal education of women and have attempted to raise the marriage age of girls. Like most reform movements, it was split and now has several branches. Like other reform movements, it has had indirect influence out of proportion to its small numbers.

VEDANTA OR RAMAKRISHNA movement in the 1890's. In many nations, including the U.S.A., it is called the Vedanta Society. It was begun by the mystic and seer, Ramakrishna Paramahamsa, who taught the unity of all religions, saying that all had the same ultimate goal. One of his followers, Vivekananda, organized a movement at Belur, near Calcutta, on the Ganges, where a set of buildings was erected. It is a movement stressing both mysticism and social action. Its leaders wish to make their religion a practical force in the community. They build schools, hospitals, and other institutions. Going into other nations, the movement has been missionary in outlook.

INTERNATIONAL CHURCH OF THE FOURSQUARE GOSPEL. This is the name of a denomination organized by Aimee Semple McPherson in Los Angeles in 1927. She started Angelus Temple as a local place of worship there in 1923, after engaging in evangelistic activities during World War I. The denomination reports almost 600 local branches in the United States, with over 80,000 members. The denomination emphasizes evangelical Protestant doctrines, with special attention to divine healing. (CRB and YBAC)

ISLAM. This is the name of the religion founded by Muhammed, also spelled Mohammed (about 570-632 A.D.). He gave the religion its name. The followers of this religion call themselves Muslims, and are also called Moslems in the Western world. They do not use "Mohammedan," a term popularly circulated. The name of God is Allah.

Islam has influenced the social systems of a score of nations. It exacts of its adherents abstinence from wine, and some strict groups abstain from all use of alcohol and tobacco. There is no professional priesthood in Islam. Images are forbidden. Islam has developed to a high state the arabesque form of architecture and ornament.

Islam is the religion of a variety of races and nations. In India and Pakistan there are about 100,000,000 Muslims; in the Arab nations of the Middle East, 65,000,000; in Indonesia and the Malay states, 70,000,000; in Turkey, 20,000,000; in Afghanistan, 12,000,000; in the Soviet Union and China, perhaps 30,000,000; in Africa outside of Egypt, 24,000,000. In all, Islam has about 350,000,000 adherents, close to one-eighth of the people of the world. Possibly the numbers are increasing at the rate of over 20,000 a year.

Historical Notes. Muhammed was born in Mecca, in Arabia. There is only a vague tradition concerning his early years. His public religious career began when he was about forty years of age. He had some knowledge of both Judaism and Christianity, which were known in Arabia. It is believed that he received ideas from these two religions which influenced his teachings on judgment, resurrection, and the future life. A dispute with the people of Mecca over idols led to his flight to Medina. This move is called the hegira, or hejira. This took place in the year 622, a date subsequently established as the beginning of the era of Islam.

Muhammed soon became the most powerful figure in Arabia and established the religion of the worship of the one God, Allah. His concept of the unity of God called for rejection of the trinitarian thought of Christianity. In addition to the unity of God he stressed the final judgment, which is to result in paradise for the true believer and hell for the unbeliever. Muhammed also drew upon the primitive religion of ancient Arabia and the customs of its people. He was a practical ruler and man of affairs who developed a religion.

Shortly after Muhammed's death, the Arab world expanded rapidly and soon had control of most of Persia and of the large Byzantine empire. The Arab tribesmen became unified by conquest and by adherence to the religion of Islam. A hundred years after Muhammed died, Islam was the religion of large numbers of people living in an area extending from Spain to India.

Muslims are probably most generally commended for their reverence for and adoration of God, and are probably viewed most critically for their practices with respect to the status of women. The prayer ritual speaks of "Allah the Merciful, the Compassionate . . . He is the High, the Mighty."

Polygamy has been an institution in many of the nations in which the people are now Muslims. Many Arabs and Asiatics defend their own legalized practice, stating that there is in it less hypocrisy than in the practice of sanctioning marital irregularities along with the profession of monogamy. They allege that their women are cared for and protected. They also state that seclusion of women as widely practiced came after the day of Muhammed and was thus not instituted by him.

Principal Beliefs and Doctrines. Prayer is required of the Muslim five times every day. This is formal and is often recited twice. It need not be a public act and may be carried on by the individual privately wherever he can arrange it. (There is a report that a devout Muslim enters a telephone booth, at the United Nations headquarters in New York, at regular intervals, faces toward Mecca and performs his act of prayer.) Prayer is one of the five pillars.

The other four are: Belief in the creed, which is simply, "There is no God but Allah, and Muhammed is the Messenger (or prophet) of Allah." More fully stated it is: "I believe in God, his Angels, his Books and his Messengers, the Last Day, the Resurrection from the dead, Predestination by God, Good and Evil, the Judgment, the Balance, Paradise and Hell-fire."

Almsgiving. This was one of Muhammed's original teachings. It has taken the form of a special levy upon the adherent for relief of the poor and other purposes. Voluntary almsgiving, in addition to the compulsory tax, is also urged.

Fasting. This is a systematic and rigorous custom once a year during the lunar month of Ramadan. In that entire month, the Muslim may not eat or drink during the day, but may do so at night. At intervals, Ramadan comes in the summer, because of the lunar calendar. When the fast is observed fully, it implies great sacrifice on the part of the individual.

Pilgrimage to Mecca. Every Muslim who possesses sufficient means is urged to go to Mecca at least once during his life. This is a ceremonious pilgrimage in which many take part every year. It is a time to emphasize the forces that hold Islam together. It is understood that neither Jews nor Christians should have a part in the ceremony, although a few of these have witnessed it.

Islam is a missionary religion. The faithful are to act for their religion and to oppose the unbelievers. This has been regarded as praiseworthy but has also been called "war against the unbelievers." What of the well-known cry, "Slay the infidel?" Whatever the subsequent practices, Muhammed wrote: "Slay the infidel if he attacks you and will not let you practice your religion. . . . If they desist from opposing you, what is already past shall be forgiven. But if they return to attack you, the like shall be inflicted on them. Therefore fight against them until there be no opposition to idolatry and the religion be wholly God's." One of Muhammed's aims was to free his nation from idolatry.

Form of Worship. Organized worship is carried on in a mosque and is conducted by an appointed person, since there is no trained professional leadership. The principal weekly service is the prayer on Friday noon in the mosque, and at this service there is also generally an address. The Muslims always face toward Mecca when they pray. Thus all mosques are built accordingly.

The *Koran,* the book of the scriptures of Islam, contains the writings of Muhammed over a period of about twenty years. It is believed that twenty years after the death of Muhammed the *Koran* took its final and present form. The literary quality and the length of the chapters vary considerably. It includes topics such as manners, morals, law, etc. In its original language the *Koran* is poetic, but translations into English do not ordinarily convey to the Western reader the majesty of the original text. The *Koran* has been supplemented by numerous writings of the tradition of Islam, which were prepared after the great expansion of the religion into the Byzantine Empire. The writing of this tradition was a means of adapting the religion written for Arabians to other peoples.

JAINISM. This is a religion which began as a reform movement within Hinduism in India. Its followers now number about 1,500,000. By some, Jainism is regarded as a sect of Hinduism; others treat it as a distinct religion. It is understood that the Jains themselves do not regard themselves as Hindus in the strict sense.

Historical Notes. The originator was Mahavira, who lived about the time of Buddha, and who began in the sixth century B.C. a movement with many of the same emphases as those of Buddha. Both, for example, taught the doctrine of Kharma, with varying interpretations; and both taught the doctrine of rebirth. Although Mahavira taught little about God, he became, like other founders of religions, an object of worship by his followers.

Principal Beliefs and Teachings. Mahavira practised asceticism and taught that salvation must come through an austere renunciation of the world. Born of a family of great means he departed from it and wandered as an ascetic for a period of twelve years. At the end of this experience of discipline, Mahavira began to teach and preach. Afterward, twenty-three other persons, Jains, went through this rigorous training. Then people began to venerate the Jains and erected temples with images of each one of the twenty-four.

The three main principles are:

Right knowledge.

Right faith.

Right conduct.

The scriptures of this group are the *Agamas,* which give rules for the good, i.e., the monastic life. Noninjury to living things, nonviolence, are the chief ethical teachings. To some followers, this teaching is carried so far as to

avoid plowing the soil lest an earthworm be injured, to
strain all water to remove life. Thus the Jains are usually
found in trade or commerce.

It follows that the Jains are vegetarians, but they eat
butter and drink milk. Certain of the more strict will not
eat tubers that grow underground for fear that they may
consume life in minute form.

There is a religious basis to the ethical teachings. Why
should one not kill, not steal, not lie? The reason one
should refrain is that these are unnatural to the soul of
man. It is natural for the soul to refrain. By restraining
oneself from such acts one avoids bringing pain to oneself and to others.

Souls go on infinitely. The universe is also without beginning or end.

Form of Worship. Jainism offers its benefits to all with
no reference to caste. Many deities of the older faith of
Hinduism continue to be worshiped by the adherents of
Jainism, but Jina, the Victor, an early prophet, must be
worshiped both in the home and in the temples.

World Mission. The Jains have formed the World Jain
Mission, which publishes literature in English. They also
publish a magazine from Central Jain Publishing House,
Ajitashram, Lucknow, India.

JEHOVAH'S WITNESSES. Jehovah's witnesses call
themselves "primitive Christians." They number over
625,000 persons throughout the world, of whom about one
third are in North America. There are over 14,000 local
congregations, of which about 3,200 are in the United
States, and 700 in Great Britain. They report being active
in practically all the nations of the world. This body reports 190,000 members in the United States, 32,000 in

Great Britain, and 12,000 in Canada. (Yearbook of Jehovah's Witnesses, Brooklyn, N.Y. 1956.)

Historical Notes. The movement is one of the native American religious developments. The Jehovah's witnesses was founded by Charles Taze Russell in Allegheny, now a suburb of Pittsburgh, Pa., in 1872. It is reported that "a few Christian persons met together in a little house in Pennsylvania to consider the Scriptures relative to the coming of Christ and His Kingdom." In 1909 the headquarters was moved to Brooklyn, N.Y., which continues to be the center of vast publishing and other activities.

Charles Taze Russell had been a Presbyterian and a Congregationalist, but became shaken in his faith. He made contact with Adventists (which see) and found that because of their belief in the second coming of Christ, this was one group he did not condemn.

Principal Beliefs and Doctrines. Jehovah's witnesses believe that the Scriptures clearly teach that the Old World ended in 1914 A.D., and that the Lord Jesus Christ is proceeding to the establishment of the new earth. . . . The Lord's next great act will be the destruction of Satan's organization and the complete establishment of righteousness on earth. . . . Under the Kingdom the people of good-will that survive Armageddon shall carry out the divine mandate to "fill the earth" with a righteous race.

Thus the Government of God, which is to continue forever, will be on earth. There will be an end to misrule and oppression, and there will be eternal peace on earth. All present governments are regarded as hopeless. Jehovah's witnesses generally refuse military service. They declare they are not pacifists but neutrals.

Form of Worship. In the local, basic unit people are

enrolled for worship, study, and numerous activities. The head of this group is known as the "congregation servant." The place of worship is called a Kingdom Hall, never a church. The services held in the Kingdom Hall match the austerity of its furnishings. All are welcome at worship, and no collection is taken. The witnesses practice the rites of baptism and the Lord's Supper. They conduct anticlerical activities. They are openly critical of all the established branches of Christendom.

Form of Organization. The witnesses are organized in seventy-one branches, of which the largest is in Brooklyn. Another active branch is that in London. The witnesses circulate over 60,000,000 pieces of literature yearly. They conduct large international assemblies, particularly in Europe and the United States.

The witnesses are essentially a society of ministers, but there is no ordination ceremony. Ministers are trained, not in theological seminaries, but in classes maintained by the local congregations. They scorn political activity.

JUDAISM. Judaism is the religion of the Jewish people, numbering about 12,000,000 in the world, of whom nearly half are in the United States. Jews in the United States number about 5,500,000; in other American nations, 500,-000; in Europe, 3,500,000; in Asia, 1,650,000; in Africa, 700,000; in Australia and New Zealand, 60,000. In general practice, a person born of Jewish parents is considered within the Jewish congregation unless he separates himself from it.

Historical Notes. The central figure in the early development of Judaism in Palestine was Moses. It was he who taught not only monotheism but ethical monotheism. The code of Moses actually set up objectives for an ideal commonwealth. It also enunciated rights of man, under the inspiration of God. "Six days shalt thou labor." "On the seventh day thou shalt rest." This limitation on the hours of labor was extended by the code of Moses to include compulsory holidays. The wages of the persons hired may not be withheld; they must be paid at the end of the day's work.

In the code, respect for the rights of property is taught, but property rights are limited. The harvest is given by God for the use of his children. Part of the harvest must be given to the helpless. Social justice is an expression of love. And when the people disregarded the high teachings of the code, a unique group of men arose, the prophets, who called the people back to the profession and practice of the religious laws. The prophets declared that the Creator was a God of justice who required of his followers that they practice social justice among themselves. Later, the rabbis carried on the teaching that true religion expresses the love of God through love of neighbor and social justice.

Principal Beliefs and Teachings. Judaism is usually thought of as a way of life, with no official articles of faith or rigidly defined creed to which the individual must give precise allegiance. Judaism has, however, a number of teachings or doctrines which throughout the ages have been considered binding upon the adherents.

God is one. This is the fundamental affirmation of Judaism. God has no limitations of form; he is unique, omnipotent, omniscient. God is the creator of the universe and also a power making for righteousness in human affairs. God is the preserver of the world. He rules the world and is the arbiter of its ultimate destiny.

The Jew is expected daily to declare: "Hear, O Israel:

The Lord our God, the Lord is One." Thus a Jew may not be compromising in his attitude toward idolatry or polytheism. Judaism stands vigorously against any dilution of the dogma of pure monotheism—against what its leaders regard as dualism in the East and trinitarianism in the West.

God is holy and the ideal of moral perfection. He is the God of mercy and love. Also, God is father of man and man's eternal Redeemer. God is nearer to man than any other source of help can be. He appears to man in time of need.

The doctrine of the unity of the human family follows from that of the unity of God. "God created man in His own image" and also made him "but little lower than the angels." All the races of the earth constitute one human family. The world is good and is ruled by God with eternal wisdom and kindness. There was no principle of evil in creation. Sin is an act of error from the right path.

There is no mediator between God and man. All persons may attain to immortal life by leading the good life —thus immortality is the reward of God for the individual's righteousness. In this regard there is no difference between Judaism and many other faiths.

Divine power will be so revealed and will so unfold that the perfection of humanity will be attained. There will be a divine kingdom of truth and righteousness on this earth. The Jew is called upon to pray daily that abominations will cease, and that all people will call upon God's name. There is to be a social order in which peace will prevail and the earth will be filled with the knowledge of God.

The Jewish people are unique people which shall not

cease. They are not better than other people and do not have a special share of God's love, they believe. But daily is the Jew to acknowledge that God has brought the Jewish people near to his great name, to declare His unity, and to give thanks to God. Because of the duty that God has laid upon this people, they in turn have more severe tasks than others.

Service of the Lord is required. Beliefs in the doctrines are not of value unless one lives in accord with the practical requirements of the beliefs. The duty of man is so to order his life that he shall live in accordance with the will of God. What God desires of man is outlined in the Five Books of Moses. It is called the Torah, or the Law. This is the foundation of the Jewish faith.

Among the teachings of the Torah are freedom of the human will to choose between good and evil. Man is responsible for his actions. God is provident, but God also punishes transgressions. God also hears the prayers of all alike. Man is called upon to study, and parents are called upon to educate their children. The Law sanctifies labor. Celibacy, except in rare instances, is regarded as unlawful. The care of the poor is an obligation of the community. The Jew is taught to be loyal to his country and to love his country.

Form of Worship. Each branch of Judaism prescribes its form of worship, or prayer book. The congregations aim to supply adequate facilities for worship, consisting of readings, prayers, address, music. The rabbis engaged by the congregations solemnize marriage. The congregations are also responsible for most of the religious education of Jewish children. Many congregations conduct weekday, as well as Sabbath, schools. The congregations often organize recreational activities, but the Jewish community has generally formed specialized organizations for charity, social welfare, etc.

In former centuries Jews engaged extensively in what is called missionary activity, or efforts to secure converts. Jews welcome converts to Judaism, and in the U.S.A. there are reported to be about 2,500 such every year. People generally become converts to Judaism in connection with marriage to a Jewish person. In the Jewish congregation no distinction is drawn between a born Jew and a convert. There are Jews who advocate more active missionary activity.

Form of Organization. The activities of the Jewish religious congregations are one form whereby the Jewish community functions. The aim of the community is to form organizations needed for social, educational, charitable, and religious needs. The congregations are specially responsible for worship and religious education, but in practical terms their activities are not separate from those of the community.

There are three branches of Judaism: Orthodox, Conservative, and Reform. The Jewish congregations follow what is known as the congregational form of government; that is, each congregation is an independent unit. There is no synod or hierarchy. The rabbis receive their ordination from one or more rabbis.

A congregation consists legally of a number of corporate members. New congregations are formed when interested Jews in a neighborhood realize the need for a congregation.

Interest in Palestine. The interest of Jews in Palestine is almost universal and has been manifested for ages. For generations American Jews have been deeply interested in the welfare of Jews in other countries. This has taken the form of work and contributions for the restoration of Palestine, and activities for relief and protection from injustices to Jewish minorities in many parts of the world. Since the establishment of the nation of Israel in a portion of Palestine in 1948, American Jews have made substantial contributions and loans to that nation and have furnished much technical assistance.

LATTER-DAY SAINTS. The Church of Jesus Christ of Latter-day Saints is one of the few distinctly American religious movements. The formation dates from 1830, when the Church was founded by Joseph Smith, a native of Vermont, at Fayette, Seneca County, New York. The Church is popularly named Mormon.

In the U.S.A. there are about 1,240,000 members. There are about 40,000 members in Canada; 50,000 in the South Pacific; and an additional 150,000 in other nations throughout the world. (Of these 150,000, one-fourth are in Mexico and three-fourths in Western Europe, according to data received from the headquarters in Salt Lake City, Utah.)

Historical Notes. Ten years prior to 1830, Joseph Smith, when fourteen years of age, had become deeply interested in the salvation of his soul and in the true church of Christ. He was much disturbed by the number of denominations then already active on the American scene and also by the numerous interpretations being made of sections of the Scripture by various churches.

Once while in a wood near his father's home, he reported that he "had a vision of great light, and two glorious personages appeared before him and commanded him to join none of the religious sects, for the Lord was about to restore the Gospel, which was not represented in its fullness by any of the existing churches."

Three and a half years later Joseph Smith received another vision during which he was instructed with respect to the second coming of Christ and his own function in regard to the coming dispensation. He was also told by an angel where he would find the plates from which the Book of Mormon was translated, and he was instructed to visit the place every year. On September 22, 1827, he related, he was permitted to receive the plates. This was after his twenty-first birthday.

There were reported to have been eleven witnesses to the fact that the plates existed. They had the appearance of gold, and included an explanation to the effect that they were the sacred records of the ancient inhabitants of this continent. Joseph Smith translated the records and dictated his translation to Oliver Cowdery, and to others, who wrote down the words.

The Translation was completed in the summer of 1829 and put into a printer's hands. A few months previous, Joseph Smith and Oliver Cowdery reported that "an angel, John the Baptist, had appeared to them and conferred upon them the priesthood of Aaron and instructed them to baptize each other by immersion." Later on, they related, three glorious beings, Peter, James, and John, conferred on them the Priesthood of Melchizedek and the keys of the apostleship. This was followed, in April, 1830, by the organization of the church at Fayette, N.Y., and a "declaration that the ancient Gospel had been restored with all its gifts and powers."

At once missionaries were sent out. The next year a colony of believers was established in Jackson County, Missouri. There was practiced the policy of segregating the converts to the new church from the "gentiles" of the community. By 1833, the presence of the colony had aroused the opposition of neighbors, who drove the Latter-day Saints from the county by mob violence.

The dispersion was marked by more violence, and Joseph Smith and his brother Hyrum were killed by a mob at Carthage, Illinois, on June 27, 1844. In 1847, there was a consolidation of forces near Omaha, Nebraska, and a strong leader, Brigham Young, was chosen president of the church. A large dissident group, however, refused to accept his leadership. (Out of these dissidents came one large group, the Reorganized Church of Jesus Christ of Latter-day Saints, with headquarters at Independence, Missouri, and several other smaller denominations.)

The opposition of the communities to the Latter-day Saints was caused in part by their advocacy of the doctrine of polygamy. This doctrine had been advanced for some years in the church, but in 1852 Brigham Young published the doctrine of celestial marriage (marriage for eternity as well as for time), including plural marriage, stating that this was based on a revelation received by Joseph Smith. This resulted in widespread public discussion throughout the nation, and in the passage by Congress of various bills forbidding plural marriages. In 1890 the head of the Latter-day Saints issued a manifesto, calling on all the Saints to "refrain from contracting any marriages forbidden by the laws of the land." Since that date such marriages have been prohibited by the Church.

Brigham Young led his followers from Illinois to Salt Lake City, which has been the headquarters of the largest Church of Latter-day Saints.

Principal Beliefs and Doctrines. The doctrines, as given by Joseph Smith, included the following: The Bible correctly translated and the Book of Mormon are both the word of God. The Saints believe in God the Father, Christ the Son, and the Holy Ghost as individual personages; in baptism by immersion for the remission of sins they hold that the same gifts that obtained in the primitive church continue today—gifts of tongues, healing, prophecy, revelation, etc. They believe that Christ will reign personally on the earth. They believe in freedom for all men to worship God in accordance with dictates of conscience.

The Latter-day Saints carry on extensive foreign missionary activities through stations in many parts of the world. They raise funds mainly through a tithing system, under which each convert is expected to pay one-tenth of his income to the church. They maintain a comprehensive welfare program to assist needy members. The church is interested in all aspects of the life of its people.

Form of Worship. Worship is conducted by a "lay ministry," i.e., the person conducting it usually has another occupation. At the Sunday service there are hymns, scripture, sermon, prayer, offering.

Form of Organization. The members of this church are organized locally into wards (corresponding to congregations or local churches). The ward has a meeting house, under the care of a bishop and two councilors. Members are now in all states of the Union. The church has a second council, or quorum, of twelve apostles who supervise the work of the church, under the chief or presiding council. The ecclesiastical organization is based upon the priesthood with its various divisions.

THE REORGANIZED CHURCH OF LATTER-DAY SAINTS. This church of Independence, Missouri, believes that the doctrine of monogamy was taught by Joseph Smith, the founder. Joseph Smith, a son of the founder, became the leader of this church in 1860. The aim of the church is to evangelize the world and to build the Kingdom of God on earth. Emphasis is laid on stewardship, the brotherhood of man, and the building of Zion. The principles of the gospel may be stated briefly as faith, repentance, baptism, laying on of hands, the resurrection, and eternal judgment. The Bible and the Book of Mormon are both regarded as the word of God. This body has 140,000 members. (YBAC)

LUTHERANS. There are about 70,000,000 Lutherans in the world. They comprise almost one-third of the Protestants in the world and about 9 per cent of the world's Christians. It is understood that there are more constituents in the Lutheran denominations than in any other family or group of Protestant religious bodies. The eighteen Lutheran denominations of the United States report 7,060,000 members. (YBAC) These bodies are the third largest family of denominations in the nation, being exceeded only by the Baptists and the Methodists.

Of the Lutherans of the world most are in Western Europe, which has about 50,000,000 constituents, according to figures published by the Lutheran World Federation, Geneva, Switzerland. Of these, the majority are in East and West Germany.

Historical Notes. Since the sixteenth century, the term Lutheran has been used to designate those Protestants whose religious faith is based in the principles enunciated by Martin Luther (1483-1546) although he was opposed to the use of the term. When it became evident to Luther, an Augustinian monk in Germany, that the reforms he thought essential could not be made within the Roman Catholic Church, he first devoted himself to matters of faith rather than of form in the new evangelical churches that arose in Germany and other nations. His was the conservative attitude among the Reformers, as distinct from the views of Zwingli and Calvin in Switzerland. Luther decided to retain altars, vestments, etc., and prepared a liturgical order of service. He also sanctioned an emphasis on preaching not practiced in the Roman Catholic Church. (For other historical data see Protestantism, below.)

Principal Beliefs and Doctrines. Lutheran bodies believe that the canonical books of the Old and New Testaments are inspired of God and are the perfect and only rule of faith and life. They believe that the three general creeds—Apostles', Nicene, and the Athanasian—exhibit the faith of the Christian Church, being in accord with the Holy Scriptures. They believe that the Augsburg Confession is in harmony with the Holy Scriptures and an exhibition of their teachings; and that the Apology, the two catechisms of Luther, the Smalcald Articles, and the Formula of Concord, are faithful developments and interpretations of the doctrines of the Word of God and of the Augsburg Confession.

"The church is the congregation of saints, in which the Gospel is rightly taught and the sacraments rightly administered." Two sacraments are recognized, baptism and the Lord's supper. These are regarded as effective means of grace and are not mere signs or memorials. Baptism of infants is the rule among Lutheran bodies; it is held to have regenerative power through which faith is begotten. When baptism is received by adults, it seals and confirms the faith begotten of the Holy Ghost through the Word.

In the Lord's Supper, according to Lutheran doctrine, the real presence of the body and blood of the Lord Jesus Christ is offered and given in, with, and under the bread and wine. They believe that the real body and blood of the Lord Jesus Christ are sacramentally and supernaturally received by those who partake of the Holy Communion.

The Lutheran faith centers in Christ as the only Saviour of sinful man. The unity of the church is primarily one of faith rather than one of organization. Justification by faith alone in Jesus Christ is held to be the central doctrine of the Word of God, in accordance with which all other doctrines are determined and developed. Preaching of the Word of God occupies a prominent function in achieving repentance and faith; preaching must be rightly divided between law and Gospel.

The Lutheran bodies require the baptized person to take instruction in the catechism preparatory to confirmation and reception of the Holy Communion. Thus only those confirmed commune. In reporting statistics these churches generally report their baptized membership, including children, and the number of communicants.

Form of Worship. As noted, Lutheran worship is liturgical, but there are no uniform rites among the numerous denominations in this large family of religious bodies. Each denomination prescribes its form of worship. Characteristic features are the large place given to congregational singing and to the importance of preaching. Luther's own hymns, such as *A Mighty Fortress is Our God*, are frequently sung. The observance of the great Christian festivals is always emphasized. Luther held that the celebration of the Lord's Supper should be the central service of the church. Certain students of liturgies write that outside of Germany the Lutheran churches became more creative in liturgy than in the land where the churches originated. In the Scandinavian nations and in America there have been notable liturgical revisions.

Form of Organization. In Europe, Lutheran church government has been influenced by the forms of political government, particularly in nations with established state churches. The Lutheran churches are "established," for example, in the Scandinavian nations and in West Germany. In Europe the prevailing authority has been from the head of the local group, through bishops, general superintendents, etc. But church procedure has been modified as political forms have become more democratic.

The ordained minister has committed to him two distinct functions—the preaching of the Gospel and the administration of the sacraments. The commitment of these functions distinguishes the minister from the laity. In the exercise of these functions all ministers are equals.

In Canada and the United States, Lutheran bodies are freely organized, independent of the state. Many Lutheran bodies of the West have been formed by immigrations from Europe, hence the numerous variations in accordance with the tradition of the church of the country of origin. In the West there are local congregations; synods often on state lines; and national bodies. The synod is as a rule the body that ordains the minister. The ceremony is performed by the president of the synod, with prayer and the laying on of hands, with the assistance of other ordained ministers. This is preceded by an examination of the candidate by a committee of the synod. Every minister is a member of the synod that ordained him, or of the synod in which he is a pastor. The minister is subject to the discipline of the synod.

The local congregation is the primary unit of organization and possesses all powers except those delegated by constitutional authority to a larger unit. The pastor and lay officers constitute the church council, which is the governing body of the local church. These lay officers are elected by the congregation.

The minister of the local church is called and elected by the voting members of the local congregation, and he usually holds indefinite tenure. The congregation may also terminate the pastoral arrangement, but dismissal of a pastor would not depose him from the ministry.

MENNONITES. The various Mennonite denominations of Canada, the United States, Alsace, Switzerland, Germany, the Netherlands, and other countries, originated in efforts in the early 1500's to recover the simplicity of the early, or Apostolic, church. There are fourteen Mennonite denominations in the United States with over 170,000 members. (YBAC) Throughout the world there are about 300,000 members. Among nations having the larger numbers are Canada with 53,000; Holland, 43,000; Germany, 12,000, according to reports furnished by the Mennonite World Conference.

There is a Mennonite World Conference with an office at Goshen College, Goshen, Ind. It is representative of Mennonite bodies throughout the world and from time to time holds meetings on subjects of common interest.

Historical Notes. The term Mennonite was first used in the year 1550, and comes from one of the leaders, Menno Simons (1496-1561), a converted Roman Catholic priest. Menno Simons was one of the leaders of a faction called the "Obbenites" after Obbe Phillips, who organized groups in Holland and North Germany.

The protests against ecclesiastical rule and organization and rigid liturgy, in favor of simple worship and form, of which the Mennonites were a part, took form in January, 1525, when a congregation of a church now Mennonite was organized in Zurich. They named themselves "Brethren" (Swiss Brethren), but were commonly known as "Täufer." One of the leaders of this group was Conrad Grebel, who had been associated with Ulrich Zwingli, the Swiss Reformer. Grebel parted with Zwingli over the issue of the independence of the church from the state.

Grebel and his co-workers opposed infant baptism. They rebaptized those persons who had been baptized in infancy. For this reason they were named Anabaptists (rebaptizers).

Although the term Mennonite dates from 1550, in Holland the people of this persuasion were called "Doopers" or Baptists. Also in Germany, Austria, and elsewhere, the name Täufer (Baptist) persisted. Certain of these Flemish Baptists emigrated to England, worked as weavers, and had a part in organizing the early Baptist movement of England.

The early Mennonites were in a difficult position, opposing both Protestant official, or state, churches and the Roman Catholic Church. Both Protestants and Roman Catholics severely prosecuted dissenters. In the Netherlands, the Mennonites were so numerous, however, by 1575, that state authorities moved reluctantly against them. Here, too, William of Orange, in 1577, ordered an end to the persecution of religious minorities. The state there no longer demanded that there be but one creed within the realm. In Switzerland, persecution, including hangings, went on into the seventeenth century.

After 1648, Mennonites were permitted to settle in the Palatinate of Germany, and many fled there from Switzerland. William Penn sought settlers from Germany, and he enlisted the Mennonite pioneers of America. They came from Crefeld, Germany, in 1683, on the ship *Concord*, to Philadelphia and settled in Germantown. From here the Mennonites soon spread north and west.

As they pushed out into the wilderness, they put into practice their principles of nonresistance, alleging that these were better protection than rifles. There are said to be few instances of injury inflicted on Mennonites by the American Indians.

Principal Beliefs and Doctrines. For doctrine, it is believed that most Mennonites accept "A Declaration of the Chief Articles of Our Common Christian Faith," compiled at a Conference in Dort, Holland, 1632. This statement containing eighteen articles was also later accepted by the Alsatian Mennonites, and by most American Mennonite Churches. Portions of a summary follow:

"The law of Christ is contained in the Gospel, by obedience to which alone humanity is saved.

"Repentance and conversion, or complete change of life, without which no outward obedience to Gospel requirements will avail to please God, is necessary to salvation. . . .

"By partaking of the Lord's Supper the members express a common union with one another and a fellowship of love for and faith in Jesus Christ.

"The washing of the saints' feet is an ordinance instituted, and its perpetual observance commanded, by Christ. . . ."

The Declaration says: "Christ has forbidden His followers the use of carnal force in resisting evil and the seeking of revenge for evil treatment. . . ." Mennonites generally are conscientious objectors to military service.

Form of Worship. The local congregations carry on informal types of worship, consisting of hymns, prayer, reading of scripture, preaching. They practice baptism, and, as before said, the Lord's Supper and the washing of feet.

Form of Organization. The form of church government, with exceptions, is congregational. Thus the local congregation is autonomous. Appeals may be taken to district conferences. Decisions of district conferences are referred back to the local congregation for ratification. The various denominations have their own bishops, ministers and deacons. The ministers are often persons who are self-supporting, i.e., persons who follow another occupation which brings them their income.

AMISH. Conservative or Old Order Mennonites go under the popular term Amish, from Jacob Amman, or Amen, a young bishop of Alsace, who led a movement for strict obedience to Menno Simon's teachings and literal interpretation of the Declaration of Dort. They hold meetings and church services in homes and other private buildings. They also prescribe a distinct mode of dress. Most of the Amish are farmers and are noted for skillful cultivation of the land. They are generally opposed to centralized schools and to formal schooling beyond certain grades. They do not associate with other bodies in religious work. They draw strict lines between themselves and other bodies. They exercise severe discipline over their members and are strict in the exercise of the ban, or shunning, of expelled members. (In 1906, two of the conferences called Amish united with the Mennonite Church, one of the largest of the Mennonite bodies.)

METHODISTS. The people called Methodist number about 30,000,000 in the world, of whom about 12,000,000 are in the twenty-two Methodist bodies in the U.S.A. Of these, the Methodist Church reports 9,300,000 members. (YBAC) There are about 900,000 in the Methodist Church in Great Britain. (WCH) In Canada, the Methodists joined with other bodies to establish the United Church of Canada in 1925.

Historical Notes. The foundations of Methodism were laid by John Wesley, who lived and died a clergyman of the Church of England. "It was not a new doctrine, but new life, the first Methodists sought for themselves and for others," wrote Wesley. He and his followers wished to maintain and extend personal Christian experience, and their system of organization was shaped by this aim.

The Methodist churches of all lands trace their origin to a movement started at Oxford University in 1729, when John and Charles Wesley, George Whitfield, and others, met for religious exercises. They read the Bible carefully and concluded that they "could not be saved without holiness, they followed after it, and incited others so to do," as Wesley put it. Soon various terms of derision were hurled at those who met. Since they wished to live by a "certain method," the name Methodist was one of these terms. Others were "Holy Club" and "Bible Bigots." The unfriendly term Methodist seems, however, to have been readily accepted by the members of the group.

Ten years later, in 1739, Wesley records, eight or ten persons came to him in London and asked that he spend some time with them in prayer. This was the beginning of what was then called The United Society. Soon the Wesleys came to know Moravians in London, in America, and in their headquarters at Herrnhut, Saxony. These conversations led John Wesley to a new understanding of saving faith and are believed to have been the source of much of the spiritual power of the movement. They were also the beginning of a chapter of his life which is known as his "heart-warming experience." There is recent evidence that the chapel in Aldersgate Street, London, which meant so much to Wesley, was a gathering place of Moravians. Wesley wrote concerning May 24, 1738:

> In the evening I went very unwillingly to a society in Aldersgate Street, where one was reading Luther's *Preface to the Epistle to the Romans*. About a quarter before nine, while he was describing the change which God works in the heart through faith in Christ, I felt my heart strangely warmed. I felt I did trust in Christ, Christ alone for salvation; and an assurance was given me that He had taken away my sins, even mine, and saved me from the law of sin and death.

After this Wesley was "a different man."

Soon Wesley found churches closed to him. The Bishop of Bristol forbade him to preach in any church of the diocese. At the church in Epworth, in which his father had been the rector, Wesley found himself "locked out" by the rector.

Then Wesley stood upon his father's tombstone in the churchyard at Epworth and spoke to an assembly on the text: "The Kingdom of God is not meat and drink; but righteousness, and peace, and joy in the Holy Ghost."

"The world is my parish" was Wesley's answer to his critics. His future ministry was to be outside the churches among the people. The closing of a thousand church doors became for John Wesley a thousand reasons why he should preach in barns, homes, and fields. His brother Charles was also excluded from pulpits. The preaching and singing of the Wesleys started a religious revival in England in the eighteenth century.

As converts were received, they were organized into societies for worship, to be followed by class meetings for the care and training of members. Then the circuit system was established, whereby several local groups were put under the care of one lay preacher. Then in 1744, the annual conference was inaugurated, in which Mr. Wesley met all his co-workers. Thus the principal features of the characteristic Methodist organization grew out of the necessities of the situation and the necessities of the early work.

Principal Beliefs and Doctrines. The doctrinal position of these congregations was in accord, in the main, with that of the Church of England. The early Methodists accepted the articles of religion based largely upon those of the Church of England, but accepted only the Apostles' Creed. The stricter doctrines of Calvinism were put aside, and in their place the warmer Arminian teaching concerning man's free will and God's grace, although George Whitfield remained a Calvinist. The Methodist churches emphasize a belief in the Trinity, the fall of man and his need for repentance, freedom of the will, sanctification, future rewards and punishments, and the sufficiency of the Scriptures for salvation.

Form of Worship. In the Methodist churches the form of worship varies considerably. It may be the simplest congregational type; or it may be what has been described as an Anglican evangelical service. In certain churches of the English-speaking world, Wesley's revisions of the *Anglican Book of Common Prayer* may be used for both morning and evening service on Sundays. The Anglican Order of Holy Communion, as revised by Wesley, is the normal form of celebration in Methodist churches of the world. The people come forward to the altar rail to communicate. The sacraments of baptism and the Lord's supper are recognized.

Form of Organization. In 1784, Wesley ordained Thomas Coke to be superintendent of the Methodist societies in America. Coke had also been ordained by the Church of England. Wesley also ordained Alexander Miller, who had not been episcopally ordained, to be superintendent of the societies in Great Britain.

In Great Britain the conference remained supreme, and the superintendency was less emphasized than in America. In America came numerous separations from the original body because of dissatisfactions with features of the original organizations. However, other denominations, notably the United Brethren bodies, were greatly influenced by Methodist principles.

In 1792 at a General Conference, the followers of Wesley formed the Methodist Episcopal Church. The order of worship and the articles of religion prepared by Wesley were adopted, with the addition of one article recognizing allegiance to the United States of America. In 1830, the Methodist Protestant Church was organized as the outcome of a movement against episcopal authority; and in 1845, the Methodist Episcopal Church, South, was formed because of anti-slavery agitation in the Methodist Episcopal Church. In 1939, these three bodies merged to form The Methodist Church, the largest Protestant body in the United States. The World Methodist Council has an office at Lake Junaluska, N.C.

MORAVIANS. The religious bodies named Moravian trace their origin to the leadership of the martyrs John Hus, in Prague, 1415, and Jerome of Prague, 1416. There are some 265,000 members in the world, of whom over 60,000 are in the United States, 3,000 in Great Britain, 1,500 in Canada, 25,000 on the continent of Europe, and the remainder in some 165 mission stations and congregations. (*Directory of the Moravian Church,* Bethlehem, Pa., 1956.)

Historical Notes. The spiritual followers of Hus organized in 1457 an association near Kunewald, in Bohemia, for the purpose of fostering pure scriptural teaching and apostolic discipline. This union grew despite opposition. It is estimated that by the time of Martin Luther in Germany, the Brethren in the union formed at Kunewald had some 400 local congregations, with some 150,000 souls as constituency in Moravia and Bohemia. But the Thirty Years' War practically devastated the region, and at its close in 1648 the evangelical churches in Moravia and Bohemia had mostly ceased to function. Some followers fled to Hungary, Saxony, Holland, and Poland.

In 1722 there was a resuscitation when a small company of followers settled on the estate of Nicholas Louis, Count of Zinzendorf, in Saxony, where the village of Herrnhut arose. In 1735, the historic Moravian episcopate was transferred to the new group, and the Unitas Fratrum, or Church of the Brethren, known in England and the United States as the Moravian Church, was established. The chief purpose of the church was to carry on evangelistic work in both Christian and other lands. In 1749, an act of the British Parliament recognized the Moravian Church as an "ancient Protestant and Episcopal Church." It has remained a comparatively small body. It has done certain undenominational work in the hope of developing an evangelistic alliance. In 1957 there is being celebrated 500 years of continuous history of what is being called the first Protestant international church.

In the United States, Bethlehem, Nazareth, and Lititz, in Pennsylvania, and Salem (now part of Winston Salem) in North Carolina, were among the communities organized as Moravian settlements.

Principal Beliefs. The Moravian Church has no doctrine peculiar to itself. It is simply and broadly evangelical, in harmony with Protestants generally. While it has no official creed, digests of teachings are found in reports of synods and in the liturgies of the church, e.g., the one used on Easter Sunday. The church accepts the Holy Scriptures as an adequate rule of faith and practice.

Form of Worship and Organization. The church follows a liturgical form of worship, with litanies prepared for regular services and for all special days and observances. It is in form of government "conferential." The church is mainly known for the mission stations it has supported and organized among the primitive people of the world.

MORMON, *see Latter-Day Saints*

MUSLIM, *see Islam*

NAZARENE, CHURCH OF. The Church of the Nazarene arose out of revivals of the 1890's. Formal organization at Pilot Point, Texas, in 1908, was a process of bringing together a number of previous movements which extended back to the 1890's. In those years there were a number of efforts for the spread and conservation of scriptural holiness. In intensity these revivals have been compared to those of the days of Wesley (see Methodists). The great impulse in the nineties was the emphasis placed by the Scriptures upon the teaching that in the atonement Jesus Christ made provision not only to save men from their sins but also to perfect them in love. The name Church of the Nazarene was formally adopted in 1919.

In November, 1901, the movement took form in Great Britain, when churches were organized in and about Glasgow. These resulted in 1915 in the formation in Scotland of the Church of the Nazarene.

The Nazarenes are essentially in accord with the historic doctrines of Methodism, which see. They stand for simplicity in worship, and pentecostal power in experience. They believe that Jesus baptizes believers with the Holy Spirit, cleansing them from all sin and empowering them to witness the grace of God to men.

This experience is known by various terms representing its different phases, such as Christian perfection, perfect love, heart purity, baptism with the Holy Spirit, Christian holiness. Followers adhere to the Biblical doctrine of divine healing.

Over 270,000 members reside in the United States. (YBAC) They conduct extensive foreign missions and support seven colleges in the United States.

NEW JERUSALEM, CHURCHES OF, (SWEDEN-BORGIAN). The Church of the New Jerusalem, also known as the "New Church," was first organized in London, 1787. It was based on the writings of Emanuel Swedenborg, prominent Swedish scientist, who turned to the study of theology. He devoted the latter part of his life to writing and interpreting concerning the revelations he reported were given to him. Among his later writings were *The Apocalypse Revealed* and *The True Christian Religion*. Swedenborg is regarded by his followers as a "divinely illuminated seer and revelator." He gave in the science of correspondences "the key" to interpretation of the Bible.

In Great Britain there are over 7,000 members. In the United States there are two denominations: The General Convention of the New Jerusalem in the U.S.A., Boston, Mass., dating from 1792, with over 4,250 members, and The General Church of the New Jerusalem, Bryn Athyn, Pa., dating from 1890, with five churches and 1,750 members. (YBAC)

The doctrines include the teaching that there is one God, the Saviour, Jesus Christ. In Him there is a trinity, not of persons, but of essence—Father, Son, and Holy Spirit. Thus the Lord Jesus Christ is the one God of heaven and earth and the object of worship of angels and of men. It is taught that when a man dies he is raised up in his spiritual body in the spiritual world, and he will live there, either in heaven or hell, depending upon the character he achieved in this world. There are voluminous other cardinal points on divine order and divine providence. Baptism is administered either to infants or to adults.

OLD CATHOLIC CHURCHES. Old Catholic Churches were organized by Dutch and Swiss theologians who refused to subscribe to the doctrine of papal infallibility enunciated by the Roman Catholic Vatican Council of 1870. The same steps were taken by local groups in Poland, Belgium, and the U.S.A. All of these churches are now relatively small, and those in Holland and Switzerland alone seem to have maintained stability.

There are four Old Catholic Churches in the United States with a total of 100,000 members whose leaders report some past connection with Old Catholic movements in Europe, and it is understood that the latter take no responsibility for any of the churches in the U.S.A.

Two churches not labeled Old Catholic nevertheless have been in direct contact with the Old Catholics of Europe. One of these is the Polish National Catholic Church, Scranton, Pa., organized in 1904 among former parishes of the Roman Catholic Church in the United States with Polish people as members. This Church has over 265,000 members. (YBAC)

The other is the Lithuanian National Catholic Church, organized at Scranton, Pa., in 1914. This body has over 5,600 members. (YBAC)

PENTECOSTAL CHURCHES. The term Pentecostal Churches or Assemblies is used to designate a group of churches emphasizing the outpouring of the Holy Spirit, sanctification, signs of supernatural forces at work, and missionary work. There is a World Conference of International Pentecostal Churches, with headquarters at Springfield, Missouri. In the United States there are nine of these denominations with about 320,000 members.

The largest of these bodies are the Pentecostal Assemblies of the World, Indianapolis, 60,000 members; the Pentecostal Church of God of America, Joplin, Mo., 60,000 members; the Pentecostal Holiness Church, Memphis,

Tenn., 47,000 members; the United Pentecostal Church, St. Louis, Mo., 125,000 members.

PRESBYTERIANS. The Presbyterian churches have the features, doctrinal and governmental, emphasized by John Calvin and his associates. They were developed in Switzerland, France, Holland, the Palatinate, England, Scotland, and Ireland. Along with the Reformed Churches (which see) holding the Presbyterian system there are about 125 denominations of this group in the world with over 41,000,000 constituents. (WCH) The distinctively Presbyterian churches in the U.S. trace their origins chiefly to Great Britain. The Church of Scotland (Presbyterian) is the established, or state, church of Scotland.

In the U.S.A. there are eleven Presbyterian denominations with over 3,860,686 members (YBAC), making them the fourth largest family or group of denominations in American Protestantism. In Great Britain there are seven bodies with over 2,000,000 constituents. The government census in Canada of 1951 reported 780,000 Presbyterians.

There is an Alliance of the Reformed Churches Throughout the World Holding the Presbyterian Order, Geneva, Switzerland.

Historical Notes. John Calvin (1509-64) was born at Noyon, France, and received a full professional education for the law, after a brief career in the Roman Catholic priesthood. His identification with the Protestant Reformation resulted in his influencing the thought of a large portion of the persons living in Western Europe and the United States. He experienced a sudden conversion in 1533 and became a partisan of the Reformation. Because of the danger of living in France, he sought refuge in

Switzerland, and in Basel, in 1536, he completed his famous work, *The Institutes of the Christian Religion.* After a series of vicissitudes in Geneva, he was invited in 1541 to make changes in the government and social life there. He made a model social code in which the church had great authority. Here Calvin wrote catechisms and a liturgy and introduced liturgical singing of the Psalms on a wide scale in the churches.

The severity of the discipline in Calvin's Geneva is frequently remarked. The burning of Michael Servetus, in 1533, is generally condemned. But Calvin was a man who pursued lofty aims with consistent purpose.

Today the term Calvinism is used with several different meanings. It may be used to denote Calvin's original theological teachings, which came in part from Augustine and Luther, and which were to become essential factors in many denominations, including those not Presbyterian and Reformed. It may refer to the development and modification of Calvin's thought by the churches having the Presbyterian system, and others. It may be used simply to designate the Presbyterian system of church government.

Calvin taught that the redemption of man must be achieved through regeneration by the power of the spirit of God "in the souls of the elect and of them alone." It is the free gift of the grace of God to those predestined to receive it, is not merited by man, and cannot be attained by good works. The Scriptures are the norm of doctrine. The sacraments are regarded as symbols of grace. The Lord's Supper provides in essence a covenant of spiritual influence. It is more than a memorial, as Zwingli, another Reformer, taught. The covenant is different from the view of Luther who held that in the Lord's Supper there is a real bodily presence. The chief end of man, said Calvin, is to glorify God, to know Him and to do His will.

Calvinism has, of course, been developed and interpreted. In various schools of thought, in many denominations, came "moderates"; e.g., those who held that man's regeneration came in part by certain appointed means, as the reading of the Scriptures and prayer, which would turn the heart away from sin and toward holiness. Others were called "consistent Calvinists," who held that man could do nothing until the spirit changed his heart, giving him a volition to turn to God. Significant "confessional conflicts" developed in the churches of the Western world over interpretations of the leader's teachings.

Principal Beliefs and Doctrines. Presbyterian churches generally emphasize as fundamental principles the undivided sovereignty of God in His universe, the sovereignty of Christ in salvation, the sovereignty of the Scriptures in faith and conduct, and the sovereignty of the individual conscience.

Forms of Worship. Among the large number of Presbyterian denominations in the world, worship takes many forms. In the Associate Presbyterian Church of North America, e.g., psalms are used in services of praise, and closed communion is practiced, i.e., the elements of the Lord's Supper are offered only to members of that body. In the Presbyterian Church in the U.S.A., the directory of worship makes no restriction as to place or form. It issues a book of worship for optional use. This church insists on the supreme importance of the spiritual element and leaves to ministers and people the right to worship in accordance with the dictates of conscience. Authorities consulted believe that this attitude is general throughout Presbyterianism.

In the Presbyterian Church of England, the directory of worship is a semi-liturgical compilation, but use of it is not obligatory except at ordination of the clergy. It provides a standard to which practice to some extent approximates. In Scotland, in the early days of the Reformation, formal standards of worship were prescribed. By the latter half of the nineteenth century there had set in a neglect of formal worship, and prescribed services fell into disuse. Since 1920 there has been a revival of liturgical worship and a movement to attain more formal standards. Thus the reunited Church of Scotland has as its standard of worship a compilation, *The Book of Common Order,* prepared in 1928.

Form of Organization. The Presbyterian system of government holds that ministers are co-equal. The authority of the church is vested, not in individuals, but in representative courts: the session of the local church; the presbytery, an association of local churches; and the synod, or, in larger bodies, the General Assembly. All these church courts are invested with executive, legislative, and judicial functions. Presbyterians make much of this principle of coordinate representative authority, by which the individual member of a local church has his own share in the conduct of that church, recognizing the headship of Christ and the fellowship in Christ. They hold that the system has modified both individualistic and hierarchical tendencies in church government. The presbyteries ordain the candidates for the ministry. Persons applying for church membership are examined by the session concerning their Christian life and belief.

PROTESTANT EPISCOPAL CHURCH, *see Anglicans.*

PROTESTANTISM. One of the three large branches of Christianity, with some 225,000,000 adherents in nearly all nations of the world, is Protestantism. Its limits are variously defined. How many and which churches should be included? Opinions differ. Probably some 230 denominations in the U.S. are commonly regarded as Protestant. The term is defined in positive terms as testimony for certain beliefs and emphasis, e.g. on Biblical authority, the priesthood of all believers, the minister as only the first among equals, advocacy of freedom for all religions, etc.

In somewhat negative terms, Protestant churches are often classified as those Christian bodies not in the Roman Catholic, Old Catholic, and Eastern Orthodox groups. This would obviously include the Spiritualists and certain groups whom others would not regard as Protestants.

The Protestant Reformation is often dated from 1517 A.D., in Germany, when Martin Luther, an Augustinian monk, challenged the current practices of the Church with respect to indulgences. On October 31 of that year Luther posted his famous ninety-five *Theses* on the door of the Cathedral in Wittenberg, Germany. From that event flowed a series of forces that resulted in the formation of new churches and the beginning of the era of Protestant denominations. Luther was accused of heresy and tried at the Diet of Worms in 1521. He began to challenge the established church more broadly than on indulgences and found himself the leader of a great schism.

Luther was the practical leader of a movement that was the beneficiary of the influence of a number of protests and ferments. There were Protestant movements before

Luther—e.g., the groups in Moravia that followed John Hus, who died in 1415, and that which was known as the Unitas Fratrum (Unity of the Brethren) in 1457. The Unity of the Brethren was obviously Protestant before the more extensive forces that came into operation after 1517.

Luther's was a powerful voice of protest. But it also spoke at a time when the stirrings of modern nationalism rocked the medieval world, when secular rulers were anxious to throw off alleged ecclesiastical controls, when there were intellectual revolts against traditional scholasticism, when the personal experiences of mystics were here and there exalted against the formalism of liturgy.

In a short time there was not one movement but many. In the U.S.A. these are *often* classified into four groups: 1. Lutheran; 2. Calvinist (Presbyterian and Reformed); 3. Anglican,* called Episcopalian in the U.S.A.; and 4. one hard to define and variously named such as "independent" or "free." Within this fourth type, however, there are various forms of government and systems. Many of these churches are "congregational" in form of government, that is, the local congregation has practically full control over its own affairs and cannot be instructed by any other body. These would include the large number of Baptist, Congregational, and Disciples churches of the U.S.A. and other nations. There are far more of the fourth type of Protestants in the U.S. than of any other. (See the various separate statements on the main groups, or "families," of Protestantism.)

Originally the Reformers were conservative with respect

* Many Anglicans request that they be not included among Protestants. But in the U.S.A., the Anglicans (the Protestant Episcopal Church) are in most reference works so classified.

to changes in doctrine. The authority of the Bible was declared, but this led to difficulties of interpretation. Every believer should approach his God without a mediator—there would thus be a priesthood of all believers. But under Calvinism and Lutheranism and Anglicanism, and elsewhere, came regulations with respect to the ministry. Thus it has been observed that the Protestant minister in actual practice is not always only the first among equals. Religious liberty has been advocated, but not uniformly throughout history, although there is now much evidence that religious liberty generally is broad where Protestantism is extensive.

Most Protestants (except those professing Unitarian beliefs) affirm that God is triune and confess him in the words of the creed as "Father, Son and Holy Spirit." (For a fuller statement on the Trinity, see page 146.) Thus most Protestants are trinitarians. Protestants generally hold that God deals with man not by law but by grace. Most Protestants affirm that man should also do good works to express his gratitude to God. Protestants believe in a God who expresses a love for every human being; in eternal life with God in "the communion of saints"; in the church as a fellowship of the believers in and followers of Christ.

The Reformation itself generated various reform movements, or "protests against Protestantism." These came out of intellectual movements which in turn led to "liberal" thought and systems in Protestantism which are far at variance with the first century of Protestantism. Examples of these bodies are the Friends, Unitarians, and Universalists, which see.

A movement with an altogether different direction came within Anglicanism, in 1833, sometimes called the

Oxford Movement, or Anglo-Catholicism. This group is a party which emphasizes the Catholic tradition, aims to recover elements found in the undivided church prior to 1054, but does not acknowledge allegiance to the Pope. The members of this party, found in considerable numbers in Britain and the U.S.A., call themselves "Catholic."

Looking at the stream of history, certain observers have said that the essence of Protestantism is division. There is much evidence to sustain this broad generalization. But within the past hundred years, a counter movement of union and cooperation may be observed. This has taken various forms. One is a merger of existing churches. Examples are the formation in 1925 of the United Church of Canada by Presbyterian, Methodist, and Congregational churches; in South India in 1947, the beginning of the Church of South India, a union of Anglican, Congregational, Methodist, and Presbyterian and Reformed bodies. The Church of Christ in Japan includes about twenty formerly separate bodies, and 75 per cent of the Protestants in that nation. In the U.S., the Methodist Church, begun in 1939, was a union of the former Methodist Episcopal; Methodist Episcopal Church South; and the Methodist Protestants. (See Church Unions, in III, below.)

Protestants and Eastern Orthodox cooperate in the many practical activities of the World Council of Churches, the National Council of Churches of Christ in the U.S.A., and in other national councils of churches in other nations, and in state and local councils of churches.

These latter developments have been called part of the "Ecumenical Movement," a term only recently gaining in circulation. Ecumenical means embracing the whole world, or universal. (See Ecumenical, in III, below.)

REFORMED CHURCHES. A large group of churches of the Reformation other than the Lutheran trace their origin to Switzerland, interest in representative government, and to the labors and teachings of the reformers, Huldreich Zwingli (1483-1531), Philip Melanchthon (1497-1560), and John Calvin (1509-64). The term Reform was generally given to Protestant Churches in Switzerland, the Netherlands, and parts of Germany. The term Presbyterian (which see) is used in the British, including the Scotch, churches. In France the churches were given the name of Huguenots, while in Bohemia and Hungary they took certain national names.

There are five bodies classified as Reformed with 426,-000 members in the United States. (YBAC) The Reformed Church in America, with headquarters in New York, N.Y., reports 205,000 members. The Christian Reformed Church, Grand Rapids, Mich., also has 205,000 members.

Historical Notes. The Reformed bodies which came to America through immigration were generally Calvinistic. Their polity was Presbyterian, although they used different terms from the Presbyterian churches. They have a consistory in the local church instead of a session; a classis representative of churches in a district instead of a presbytery; and a general synod instead of a general assembly.

The work of Zwingli in Germany and Switzerland, particularly in Zurich, was altogether independent of Luther. He was ordained a Roman Catholic priest and engaged in wide study of the Scriptures and of the writings of Erasmus. Appointed to Zurich, he used his influence there to prevent the sale of indulgences. He received the support of the magistrates of the city who soon instructed all priests in the canton to follow his teachings.

By 1525 there was a complete break with the old order. In that year Zwingli observed the Lord's Supper as a commemorative feast. This emphasis was one cause of his disagreement with Luther. Zwingli persuaded Bern to join Zurich in revolt against Rome, but five other cantons disagreed. In the resulting civil war Zwingli served as a chaplain. Zwingli proposed thorough-going reorganizations of the church and the civil government. He met his death in battle. Much that he advocated, however, was later set aside in the Reformed and Presbyterian churches of the world in favor of Calvin's views.

The Reformed Church in America, one of the large Reformed bodies, dates from the formation of a church in New York in 1628. Its headquarters is at 156 Fifth Ave., New York, N.Y.

The Reformed Church in the United States, an immigration from Germany, dates from 1725. This body merged in 1934 with the Evangelical Synod of North America to form the Evangelical Reformed Church, 1505 Race Street, Philadelphia, Pa.

Principal Beliefs and Doctrines. The doctrinal standards of these churches are traced to the Belgic Confession, the Heidelberg Catechism, and the Declaration of the Synod of Dort. These confessions place emphasis on salvation through Christ as the central theme. The primacy of God and His power in human affairs are at the heart of the preaching of the church. It is declared that the final authority is the Scripture, the living word of God, available to every man through the Holy Spirit.

Form of Worship. The form of worship is often described as "semi-liturgical," although it is understood that use of the liturgy is optional. Proponents allege that in the Reformed bodies there is a blending of form and freedom. The two sacraments recognized are baptism and the Lord's Supper.

Form of Organization. The Reformed bodies follow in form of government a sort of modified Presbyterianism (which see). In the local church the governing body is the consistory, made up of elders, deacons, and the minister, who is the president. A number of local churches are grouped into a classis or district association (generally corresponding to the presbytery), which is composed of all the ministers plus one layman from each local church. The classis supervises the local churches. The various classes are then grouped in a representative manner into "particular synods." The highest court is the general synod.

THE ROMAN CATHOLIC CHURCH. The Roman Catholic Church is the largest church of Christendom, with about 475,000,000 members in the nations of the world. There are 33,500,000 in the United States; 6,250,-000 in Canada; 3,660,000 in Great Britain, including Wales; 50,000,000 in Brazil; 47,000,000 in Italy; 35,500,-000 in France; 28,300,000 in Spain; 21,000,000 in Poland; the remainder in some 125 colonies and nations. (*The National Catholic Almanac*, Paterson, N.J., 1956.)

Historical Notes. The Holy Catholic Apostolic Roman Church recognizes the Bishop of Rome, the Pope, as the Vicar of Christ on this earth, and as the Head of the Church. It traces its origin from the naming of the Apostle Peter by Jesus as the chief of the Apostles. The authority of Peter as head of the Church is exercised by his successors as the Bishops of Rome.

The doctrines of the Roman Catholic Church come from the faith given by Christ to his Apostles. That faith is sustained by the Holy Scriptures and also by the tradition of the Church. The doctrines are both defined and safeguarded by the Pope when he speaks "ex-cathedra," or as the head of the Church, and states that he is speaking as such on a matter of faith and morals.

Truths accepted by the Church are contained in the Apostles' Creed, the Nicene Creed, and the Athanasian Creed. Those who join the church must assent to a formulation of the doctrine in a "profession of faith." These must also pledge themselves to accept the teachings of the church on matters of faith and morals and promise to deny all teachings declared to be in error by the church.

Principal Doctrines. The individual member accepts the following statement:

"One only God, in three divine persons, distinct from, and equal to, each other—that is to say, the Father, the Son, and the Holy Ghost.

"The Catholic doctrine of the Incarnation, Passion, Death, and Resurrection of our Lord Jesus Christ; and the personal union of the two Natures, the divine and the human; the divine maternity of the Most Holy Mary, together with her spotless virginity.

"The true, real, and substantial presence of the Body and Blood, together with the Soul and Divinity of our Lord Jesus Christ, in the most holy Sacrament of the Eucharist.

"The seven sacraments instituted by Jesus Christ for the salvation of mankind; that is to say, Baptism, Confirmation, Eucharist, Penance, Extreme Unction, Orders, Matrimony.

"Purgatory, the resurrection of the dead, everlasting life.

"The primacy, not only of honor, but also of jurisdiction,

of the Roman Pontiff, successor of St. Peter, Prince of the Apostles, Vicar of Jesus Christ; the veneration of the saints and of their images; the authority of the apostolic and ecclesiastical traditions, and of the Holy Scriptures, which we must interpret, and understand, only in the sense which our holy mother the Catholic Church has held and does hold; and everything else that has been defined and declared by the sacred canons, and by the General Councils, and particularly by the Holy Council of Trent, and delivered, defined, and declared by the General Council of the Vatican, especially concerning the primacy of the Roman Pontiff, and his infallible teaching authority."

Baptism is administered to infants and to adults by the pouring of water, by repetition of the approved words of the ceremonial. It is a sacrament that "cleanses from original sin and initiates the life of grace in the soul." The general practice is to baptize infants. Baptism is the condition of membership, whether the person is infant or adult. On being baptized, the name of the person is recorded as a Catholic.

The Church commands its members to hear mass on Sunday and on holy days of obligation; to fast, and to abstain from meat on the days appointed; to confess to a priest at least once a year; to receive holy communion at Easter time; to contribute to the support of pastors; and to observe the regulations of the Church with respect to marriage.

Form of Worship. Mass is celebrated every day. Sunday masses are offered in the local churches, morning and evening, the high mass usually being celebrated between 10:00 A.M. and noon. Masses are offered as often as necessary to meet the needs of parishioners. At high mass

education. Most colleges and universities are also con-ducted by religious orders. It is the purpose of the Church to organize its own parochial schools for all Catholic children so that they may receive religious instruction as part of their general education and relate their religious beliefs to secular knowledge.

Home and foreign missions are aided by many organi-zations. Catholic charities are well organized. In certain dioceses all members are urged to contribute an amount equal to one day's pay annually to the diocesan charities. The Church maintains large numbers of general hospitals, homes for aged, and agencies for children.

Lay people express themselves through a wide variety of organizations, coordinated in three national units: the national councils of Catholic Men, Catholic Women, and Catholic Youth. These three councils are under the direc-tion of the National Catholic Welfare Conference.

The Church in the United States is the fourth largest in the world, being exceeded in numbers only by the Roman Catholics in Brazil, Italy, and France. During the ten years preceding 1955, over 1,000,000 adult converts were received into the Roman Catholic parishes.

Promotion of unity in Catholic work in the U.S.A. is carried on by the National Catholic Welfare Conference, Washington. (CRB)

SALVATION ARMY. This is a denomination operating in some sixty nations. In Great Britain over 1,600 centers are reported; in Canada, 1,275 centers with a constituency of 34,000 persons. (WCH) In the United States there are 1,350 centers with a constituency of over 250,000 per-sons. (YBAC)

Historical Notes. The Salvation Army comes from a

movement led by William Booth, an ordained minister of the Methodist New Connection in England. In 1865, deeply affected by the conditions of the masses in London, he organized the East London Mission. He held street meetings at which he preached to the people who he thought were living in darkness. He believed that the preaching penetrated the darkness. He sought the lost, and it was soon reported that "moral miracles" were observed. In 1878 it was stated that the "Christian Mission is a volunteer army." Soon the Mission came actually to be known as The Salvation Army.

Principal Beliefs and Doctrines. In doctrine, the Salvation Army emphasizes a holy God, a holy Bible, and a holy people. Basic to all is a right life. The love of God is as wide as the whole world. The soldier affirms that he is willingly surrendered to God. He pledges himself not to use intoxicating liquor and harmful drugs.

The Salvation Army carries on many works for the spiritual regeneration of mankind. It operates hostels and industries for the rehabilitation of needy persons. Understanding, sympathy, and advice are given to many handicapped persons, as well as material relief. (CRB)

Form of Worship. Worship is informal, consisting largely of hymns, prayer, and preaching.

Form of Government. The form of government is of a military character.

SEVENTH-DAY ADVENTIST, *see Adventists.*

SHINTOISM. This is the name of a religion observed by many people in Japan. From early days it has been known in that nation as the way of the Kami, or the Gods. There are probably about 25,000,000 followers, but many Shintoists are also Buddhists. It is an indigenous religion with two wings: one, the original, natural religion; two, a cultural religion, with ethical and intellectual characteristics.

The Two Wings. The native religion has festivals largely associated with the procession of the seasons, seedtime, and harvest. It is divided into thirteen sects or denominations. In its lower and earlier stages this Shintoism is polydemonism; in its higher stages it is polytheism. It is filled with mythology, with divine drama played by different gods and goddesses in the plain of high heaven, where the celestial beings dwell.

The cultural religion, often called the state Shinto religion, is the national faith of the Japanese people generally. It is manifested specifically in the Shrine Shinto, taught in schools as national ethics. In some respects this Shinto has developed as the national faith, with a form of morality enkindled by the fire of religion. Involved here is the Japanese brand of patriotism, including loyalty to the sovereign, with the devotion of religion.

Historical Notes. Shinto as a cultural or national religion was not consciously adopted by the rulers in the way that certain nations have established a state church. Shintoism is of the origin and life of every citizen, old and young, educated and elite. It has been stated that no Japanese ceases to be a holder of the national faith or to embrace the national faith of the way of the Gods. He may also be a Buddhist, but to be a good citizen, he must be a Shintoist. Not to do so would be blasphemy to the Divine Ruler of the nation. It is also a religion of broad toleration.

Recent Developments. But when it was expected that citizens go through certain Shinto ceremonials, some persons in other religions objected, saying that to do so would make them disloyal to their faith. This brought about difficulties. One step was to give control of state Shinto to a special Bureau of Shrines, while the sectarian Shinto was administered by the Bureau of Religion in the Department of Education.

Many changes have come with the defeat of Japan in World War II. The occupation authorities decreed that Shinto must be entirely separated from the government and receive no public support, that no officer of the government might take part in an official capacity in any of the Shinto ceremonials. Possibly most significantly, the Emperor broadcast an announcement to the people that he was a man, thus himself denying the widely held popular belief in the divinity of the Emperor.

This was followed by a period of uncertainty and confusion. One result was the formation of as many as 600 new sects in Japan. For a time the state shrines fell into disrepair, but popular support was forthcoming and attendance in the 1950's was reported to be about as wide as in the days before separation from the government. And many Shinto priests were reported to be relieved because they were no longer under the control of the state.

Observers also point to an increasing awareness of the growth of the ethical principles of uprightness and sincerity within Shintoism. Indeed, it is said that one sect has teachers akin to the prophets of Israel, teaching the virtues of sincerity, universal brotherhood, and a deity full of sympathy, responsive to sincerely offered prayer.

SIKHISM. About the time of Martin Luther's rise in Germany there lived in India a man named Nanok who

became the founder of the Sikhs, which group now numbers some 6,250,000 persons in that nation. Nanok, born
1469, studied both Hinduism and Islam, and tradition has
it that he went to Mecca in his search. The word Sikh
means disciple, or follower. Nanok's parents were orthodox Hindus, and as a boy he found himself protesting
against the rigidities of Brahmanism and the whole caste
system.

To a Brahman priest who came to initiate Nanok at
age nine into the caste of his fathers, with the sacred
thread, the boy is said to have recited a hymn containing
the following: "Make mercy Thy cotton, contentment
Thy thread, continence its knot, truth its twist."

The reformer was greatly influenced by the poet Kabir,
who was one of those who sought to work out some sort
of combination of the teachings of Hinduism and Islam.
Kabir was a man of insight who had theistic ideas. Nanok
forbade idols and invited persons from all castes into his
movement. He taught that there is but one God, the
Creator immortal, unborn, self-existent. Man attains salvation by obeying God. The praise of God is constantly
repeated in the numerous hymns. Ascetic practices were
repudiated.

Nanok regarded himself as a teacher, the Guru. On the
death of the leader, there was a succession of Gurus,
which became hereditary. The fifth of these brought together the writings of Nanok and other prayers and poems
into the Scripture of the Sikhs, named the Granth. The
movement spread and assumed the proportions of a national group. The tenth of the Gurus led an army that
conquered the Punjab, the northwestern section of India.
He also added a portion to the Granth. He began a practice of veneration of the Granth.

The division of the great sub-continent in 1950 created new problems for the Sikhs. Many of their temples happen to be in Pakistan, which is the Muslim nation, and there is hostility between Muslim and Sikh. Many Sikhs have emigrated, partly under pressure, from Pakistan to India.

SPIRITUALISTS. Spiritualism as an organized religious movement is believed to date from 1848 in the United States, and is traceable to the writings of Andrew Jackson Davis of Poughkeepsie, New York. These writings aroused interest in many nations. Thus there sprang up the organization of groups under the term Spiritualism, based on the possibility of communion between persons in this world with those who have died. In view of the fact that the established religious groups did not teach concerning the possibility of communion with those who had died, it was felt necessary to form new organizations. Spiritualists believe that the spirit world is a counterpart of the visible world, only more beautiful and perfect. They are not definitive with respect to the conventional doctrinal questions, views of God, e.g., being reported to be highly divergent.

In the United States there are three denominations with about 175,000 members. (YBAC) The Greater World Christian Spiritualist League of England reports 23,000 members (*A Christian Yearbook, London, 1950*).

SWEDENBORGIAN CHURCHES, *see New Jerusalem, Churches of*

TAOISM, *see Chinese Sages*

UNITARIANS. Unitarianism as a religious doctrine is known for a belief in the humanity of Jesus as distinguished from the Trinitarian concept of one God in three persons, Father, Son, and Holy Spirit.

In the United States, 96,000 Unitarians are reported. (YBAC) In Great Britain there are over 26,000 members in Unitarian and Free Christian Churches. (WCH)

Historical Notes. The Unitarian teaching has been believed by individuals for many centuries of the Christian era, but modern Unitarianism as a movement dates from the first fifty years of the Protestant Reformation. In England, Unitarianism as a religious body developed gradually during the eighteenth century. John Biddle (1615-62) is known as the father of English Unitarianism. In America, the Unitarian churches developed out of New England Congregationalism, when many of the churches simply required their members to join in a covenant. Thus a number of the Congregational churches of Eastern Massachusetts adopted liberal positions and were known as liberal churches in the second half of the eighteenth century. The name Unitarian was first formally taken by a church in Philadelphia in 1796.

The formation of the denomination was a most gradual process. In 1819, William Ellery Channing, a leader of liberal thought, preached a sermon which defined views held and defended by Unitarians and which became a sort of platform. The American Unitarian Association, Boston, was organized in 1825 to promote common interests of the local churches.

The American Unitarian Association and the General Convention of the Universalist Church of America formed a Council of Liberal Churches, in 1953, to promote certain common interests, including such joint projects and programs as may be committed to it by the two bodies.

Principal Beliefs and Doctrines. The Unitarians have never adopted a creed and do not require profession of any particular doctrine from their members or their ministers. A covenant reported to be often used in local churches reads: "In the love of truth, and in the spirit of Jesus, we unite for the worship of God and the service of man." (CRB)

Organization and Worship. The Unitarian churches are congregational in form of government. The local church also has full control over the form of worship. Unitarians often join in conferences with other liberal groups.

UNIVERSALISTS. As an organized religious movement, Universalism has been confined mainly to the North American continent since about 1770, although the doctrines have been held by individuals since the beginning of Christianity. In the United States there are 70,000 members. (YBAC)

Historical Notes. The first local church was built in Gloucester, Mass., in 1780, and the first steps toward denominational organization were taken at Oxford, Mass., in 1785. But it was not until a Centennial General Convention was held in 1870 that a plan of administration of the denomination was formally adopted.

Principal Beliefs and Doctrines. Universalism has been stated to be the belief that it is the purpose of God, through grace revealed by Jesus Christ, to save every member of the human race, that there is a sane and beneficent universe in which truth, right, and love are supreme.

There is a historic doctrinal symbol, the Winchester Profession, adopted in 1803, by a gathering without authority over local churches or their members. It has since been acknowledged by the denomination at large as an expression of faith. In 1903, at Worcester, the General Convention adopted a bond of fellowship, reading: "The bond of fellowship in this Convention shall be a common purpose to do the will of God as Jesus revealed it and to cooperate in establishing the Kingdom for which he lived and died." Although there is no required statement of belief, it is the judgment of Universalist writers that Universalists are generally not Trinitarians, but many hold Jesus had a unique relation to God.

Organization and Worship. The local parish or society is independent in the management of its affairs, including worship. There are state conventions and a General Convention having jurisdiction over clergymen and over denominational organizations.

VEDANTA SOCIETIES, *see Hinduism*

YOGA, *see Hinduism*

ZOROASTRIANISM.

This is the Iranian religion with adherents in parts of Iran and in India. Its followers may number 1,000,000 persons, mostly in India.

Historical Notes. Zoroaster, the founder, was born about 630 B.C. He lived in the Eastern territory occupied by the Iranian (Persian) tribes of the day, somewhere near Afghanistan.

Principal Beliefs and Doctrines. The prophet Zoroaster lived among a primitive agricultural people who were soon absorbed in the Empire of Cyrus the Great. His religion survived that cataclysm because it had the support of leaders of the Eastern Iranian tribes.

The central idea is the individuality of man and his responsibility toward the universe in which he lives. Zoroaster broke with the tradition that held that the tribe and the family were the centers of life and must be preserved. Considering the time in which he lived, Zoroaster broke boldly with the prevailing views of his time.

The individual chooses whether to ally himself with good or with evil. In the after life, the individual will be in Heaven or Hell, according to his actions on earth. Thus there will be reward or punishment.

Zoroaster also taught a moral dualism. He believed that the two highest beings were the Good God and the Evil Antitheos. God he named Ahura Mazda (Ormuzd). The Good God turned a beneficent spirit toward the world. He created everything that is true, good, wholesome, healthy, beautiful, and constructive. The name of Antitheos, the Evil Being, is taboo and is never mentioned in the Scriptures. All that is false, immoral, ugly, and destructive is the work of that Being.

Zoroaster lived at a time when monotheism was succeeding polytheism in parts of the world. And one of the problems of monotheism is that of evil—whence comes evil, why do righteous people suffer? Zoroaster posed the solution outlined above. He taught the idea of a God who is good and just, but one of limited power.

He also taught that there were beneficent immortals, associated with the Good God. These figures were in a relation to the elements or phenomena of fire, water, earth, metal, man, animals, plants, in such a way that each immortal is the spiritual counterpart of each of these material classifications.

There is only one great command of this religion: Fight for good against the evil. The result depends upon the will and resources of mankind. In terms of specifics, one should be generous to the poor, relieve those in distress, cultivate the land zealously, marry and care for children. One's attitude should be positive.

Zoroaster, like other founders of religion, taught with urgency, because he believed that the end of the world was near.

Worship. The teachings of Zoroaster are preserved in the form of poems, Gathas, included in the prayer book of the Zoroastrians, the *Yasna.* The Iranian scriptures also include numerous subsequent writings.

Organization. Zoroastrian priests minister in only a few temples of remote areas of Persia. The followers are found today mainly in the cities of India. They are highly respected for their morality and charity.

II

STATISTICAL TABLES

ONLY BRIEF summaries of compilations can be presented here. For more detail the reader is referred to the sources cited below the tables and in the preceding Note on Sources. In certain instances, only crude estimates can be cited. For example, many Buddhists are also Confucianists in China, and many Shintoists are also Buddhists in Japan.

WORLD RELIGIONS: ESTIMATES OF ADHERENTS

Christians	895,000,000
Buddhists	350,000,000
Muslims	350,000,000
Confucianists	300,000,000
Hindus	300,000,000
Taoists	50,000,000
Shintoists	25,000,000
Jews	10,000,000
Sikhs	6,250,000
Jains	1,500,000
Zoroastrianists	1,000,000

Sources: World Faith, by Ruth Cranston, New York, 1949; *Information Please Almanac,* New York, 1956; *World Christian Handbook,* London, 1952; plus figures available from the religious bodies, as noted in preceding text.

Christian Religions

Roman Catholics	475,000,000
Orthodox and other Eastern Churches	175,000,000
Copts	10,000,000
Anglicans and Protestants	235,000,000

Source: World Christian Handbook, London, 1952; plus data compiled by the author from later published figures.

Anglicans and Protestants

Lutherans	70,000,000
Presbyterian and Reformed	41,100,000
Baptists	40,000,000
Methodists	30,000,000
Anglicans	30,000,000
Congregationalists	5,000,000
Others	8,900,000
	235,000,000

Source: World Christian Handbook, London, 1952; plus data compiled from later published figures.

Religion of Canadian People

In the 1951 Census of Population conducted by the Canadian Bureau of Statistics, Ottawa, "each person was asked to state the religious body, denomination or sect to which he or she belongs or adheres," and the results were published by the Bureau in a Bulletin, *Population: Religious Denomination*, ninth Census of Canada.

Out of a population of 14,009,429, only 59,679 persons stated "No religion." The five largest groups, with the percentage of total population, were:

Roman Catholic	6,069,496	43.3 per cent
United Church of Canada	2,867,271	20.5 per cent
Church of England in Canada	2,060,720	14.7 per cent
Presbyterian	781,747	5.6 per cent
Baptist	519,585	3.7 per cent

Of these five, only the figures for the United Church and the Roman Catholic figures for 1951 represented a gain in percentage of total population, compared with 1941 and 1931.

Separate figures were published for twenty-eight bodies or groups. For example, all Lutherans were grouped together under one head.

The full list, with the precise terminology used, is as follows:

Adventist	21,398
Baptist	519,585
Buddhist	8,184
Christian and Missionary Alliance	6,398
Christian Science	20,795
Church of Christ, Disciples	14,920
Church of England in Canada	2,060,720
Confucian	5,791
Doukhobor	13,175
Evangelical Church	50,900
Free Methodist	8,921
Greek Catholic	191,051
Greek Orthodox	172,271
Jehovah's witnesses	34,596
Jewish	204,836
Lutheran	444,923
Mennonite	125,938
Mormon	32,888
No religion	59,679
Pagan	2,420
Pentecostal	95,131
Presbyterian	781,747
Roman Catholic	6,069,496

Salvation Army	70,275
Unitarian	3,517
United Church of Canada	2,867,271
Others	122,605

It is understood that certain of the religious bodies in Canada report lower figures when they reveal actual members. In the population census, evidently many "adherents" who are not active members are listed.

GREAT BRITAIN

(A listing of the reports as printed in *World Christian Handbook*, London, 1952)

Name of Body	Membership
Apostolic Church	5,300
Assemblies of God in Great Britain and Ireland	.....
Baptist Union of Great Britain and Ireland	335,640
Brethren	80,000
Calvary Holiness Church	620
Churches of Christ in Great Britain and Ireland	.....
Church in Wales	200,000[f]
Church of England	2,965,200[e]
Church of Jesus Christ of Latter-day Saints	7,386
Church of Scotland	1,273,027
Congregational Union of England and Wales	227,002
Congregational Union of Scotland	35,139
Countess of Huntingdon's Connection	1,218
Elim Church	16,000
Episcopal Church in Scotland	56,500
Free Church of England	6,300
Free Church of Scotland	.....
Free Presbyterian Church of Scotland	1,000
General Conference of the New Church	6,700
Glynn Vivian Miners' Mission	200

Name of Body	Membership
Independent Methodist Churches	7,742
International Holiness Mission	956
Lutheran Council of Great Britain	11,710
Methodist Church	741,596
Moravian Church	2,904
Presbyterian Church of England	68,562
Presbyterian Church of Wales	157,124
Reformed Presbyterian Church of Scotland	670
Religious Society of Friends	20,839
Roman Catholic Church	3,020,000[g]
Seventh-day Adventists	6,551
Union of Welsh Independents	123,563
Unitarian and Free Christian Churches	26,000
United Free Church of Scotland	24,528
United Original Secession Church of Scotland	1,901
Wesleyan Reform Union	6,299

[e] Electoral rolls.
[f] Easter communicants.
[g] Also 2,800,000 in Eire.

ROMAN CATHOLIC MEMBERSHIP STATISTICS

United States	33,500,000
Canada	6,250,000
Great Britain	3,660,000
Brazil	50,000,000
Italy	47,000,000
France	35,500,000
Spain	28,300,000
Poland	21,000,000
Other Nations and Colonies	249,000,000
	475,000,000

Source: National Catholic Almanac, Paterson, N. J., 1956.

CONTINENTAL UNITED STATES
STATISTICS OF MEMBERSHIP BY
GROUPS OF PROTESTANT RELIGIOUS BODIES

	Number of Bodies Reporting	Inclusive Membership
Adventists	5	312,782
Baptists	27	18,793,097
Brethren (German Baptists)	5	239,664
Brethren (River)	3	7,284
Churches of God	8	382,775
Churches of the New Jerusalem	2	5,980
Congregational Christian . .	1	1,342,045
Disciples of Christ	1	1,897,736
Eastern Orthodox Churches	19	2,386,945
Evangelistic Associations . .	11	39,903
Friends	8	121,468
Latter-day Saints	6	1,372,640
Lutherans	19	7,059,593
Mennonites	14	168,624
Methodists	22	11,784,060
Moravians	2	60,800
Old Catholics	4	101,491
Pentecostal	9	319,776
Protestant Episcopal	1	2,757,944
Presbyterians	10	3,860,686
Reformed	5	426,737
Spiritualists	3	173,863
United Brethren	2	20,566

Source: Yearbook of American Churches for 1957. New York, National Council of Churches, 1956. In certain groups the total number of bodies is slightly larger than the number reporting statistics for the volume cited.

CONTINENTAL UNITED STATES
MEMBERSHIP, BY RELIGIOUS GROUPS

Group	Number of Members
Buddhists	63,000
Old Catholic and Polish National Catholic	367,370
Eastern Churches	2,386,945
Jewish Congregations	5,500,000
Roman Catholics	33,396,647
Protestants (Including Protestant Episcopal)	58,448,567
Total	100,162,529

Source: Yearbook of American Churches for 1957. New York, National Council of Churches, 1956.

III

DEVELOPMENTS IN RELIGIOUS BODIES

CHURCH UNIONS. Among the recent mergers of church bodies throughout the world are the following:

THE UNITED CHURCH OF CANADA, 1925. This was a union of former Methodist, Congregational, and Presbyterian churches. A portion of the Presbyterians of the nation declined to enter the union and continued to maintain a separate body, the Presbyterian Church in Canada, Toronto. The Methodists were the largest group entering the merged. Probably about 20 per cent of those affiliated with all churches in Canada are in the United Church. The headquarters of the United Church is in Toronto.

THE CHURCH OF SOUTH INDIA, 1947. This was a merger of Anglicans and the South Indian United Church, itself a prior merger of three bodies. The movement began early in the twentieth century, with Presbyterians leading the way. In 1908 the Presbyterians and the Congregational churches united, and were joined by the Methodists in 1925. The name of the first merged body was the South India United Church. The plan for the church

formed in 1947 was first published in 1929. The headquarters of the Church of South India is in Madras. The
membership is about 335,000.

THE REFORMED CHURCH OF FRANCE, 1938. This was
formed by merging the Reformed Evangelical Church of
France, the Evangelical Methodist Church of France, the
union of Evangelical free churches, and the Reformed
Church of France. The new body thus took the name of
one of the four uniting bodies. The church reports about
200,000 members with a total constituency of 350,000 persons. The headquarters is in Paris. A large portion of
the Protestants of the cities of France are reported to be
in the united body.

THE DUTCH REFORMED CHURCH, 1946. This body united
the Dutch Reformed Church and the Reformed Churches
in the Netherlands (in Restored Connections). The body
regards itself as "confessing, apostolic, and ecumenical."
This body reports 700,000 members. The headquarters is
in Baarn, the Netherlands.

THE CHURCH OF CHRIST IN JAPAN, 1941. Fifteen denominations united, of which the largest were Presbyterian,
Methodist, and Congregational. There had been sentiment for union for many years, but the formation of the
union was hastened by action of the government of Japan
early in World War II. The government wished to reduce
the number of denominations. Also, in 1940, Christianity
was formally recognized by law, along with Shintoism and
Buddhism as one of the religions of Japan. There are
about 125,000 members. The headquarters is in Tokyo.

The Evangelical Church in Germany, 1948. Twenty-seven independent regional churches formed an organization which has been termed to be "not a church in the full sense of that word." It is nevertheless more than a confederation of independent churches. It is a church in process of coming into existence. The independent churches affiliated have no right to withdraw from the new body by unilateral action. Most of the regional churches affiliated are Lutheran. The total constituency of the Evangelical Church in Germany numbers about 40,000,000 persons. Headquarters are maintained at Hannover and Frankfurt.

The Evangelical United Brethren Church, 1946. In the United States, the Evangelical Church and the Church of the United Brethren in Christ both had their origin in missions and revivals among German immigrants. Similarities in doctrine and discipline made it relatively easy for the two bodies to unite in 1946, following discussions begun systematically in 1933. The new church has doctrinal statements which come from Methodist traditions.

Unions of churches within a family or group of denominations are referred to under the various articles on Protestant denominations. For example, the formation of the Methodist Church from three bodies, in 1939, is described under Methodists.

The (Proposed) United Church of Christ. This is a body in process of formation, which, according to published plans, will in June, 1957, unite the Congregational Christian Churches and the Evangelical Reformed Church, in the United States. It is a plan for a United

Church which other bodies are invited to join later. The proponents of the plan state that "for the first time, two great churches of different cultural backgrounds—the one Continental European, the other British—and with dissimilar forms of policy—the one presbyterian, the other congregational—will join in a common fellowship, possessed of a common responsibility to a Lord who is the Christ of the New Testament. Differences there are between them, but they are subordinated and submerged in the common evangelical character of the two uniting bodies and their common faith in the scripture interpreted in the light of its revelation of Jesus Christ." (From joint statement issued by Executive Committee, General Council, Congregational Christian Churches and General Council, Evangelical and Reformed Church, New York, 1955.)

COUNCIL OF LIBERAL CHURCHES (UNITARIAN-UNIVERSALIST). This organization was formed in 1953, with headquarters in Boston. It was organized to aid and assist the American Unitarian Association and The Universalist Church in such fields as may be assigned to it by both of these bodies. The activities of this Council may result in a union of the two denominations.

CHRISTIAN-JEWISH COOPERATION. In many nations, particularly the United States and Great Britain, systematic activities have been carried on during the past three decades toward developing the common interests of Christians and Jews in community life. These programs have taken varied forms. They have usually been initiated by laymen. In some instances clergy have inaugurated programs. In all nations where activities are carried on, there is cooperation on the part of clergymen and officials of religious bodies.

In the United States, early developments date from the appointment in 1924 of Committees in Good Will by both the Federal Council of the Churches of Christ in America, a federation of Protestant denominations, and the Central Conference of American Rabbis, the Reform branch of Judaism. For several years a number of joint activities were encouraged by these organizations.

In 1928, the National Conference of Christians and Jews was formed in New York by Charles Evans Hughes, Newton D. Baker, S. Parkes Cadman, and others. The conference has drawn together large numbers of persons, including clergy and laity in many walks of life, who have worked for democratic living, for respect and good will among all religious and cultural groups. The conference has brought together under various auspices people who have striven to create understanding and cooperation in their everyday relations as citizens.

In 1942, Dr. William Temple, Archbishop of Canterbury, took the leadership in the formation of the British Council of Christians and Jews, an organization which, in the words of Dr. Temple, would "resist intolerance and promote mutual understanding between Jews and Christians." This step followed a series of events during World War II, which created "interreligious cooperation" on a wide scale.

In 1946, there was held at Oxford, England, the first International Conference of Christians and Jews, on the initiative of the National Conference of the United States. At a conference in Paris in 1950 there was formed World

Brotherhood, which promotes understanding in many nations, through professional staff and offices at Geneva, New York, and Honolulu.

ECUMENICAL MOVEMENTS. The term ecumenical is often used to describe agencies that are international or universal. It is an old term that is applied to the series of conferences in which all of ancient Christianity participated. More recently it has been used to designate world conferences in which many Protestant and Eastern Orthodox have met, e.g., the Assembly of the World Council of Churches, Geneva and New York.

The World Council of Churches and many other international organizations representative of religious bodies in many nations are also called ecumenical.

Still more broadly, the term has been applied to all forms of cooperative activities in which local churches engage through their Councils of Churches. The National Council of Churches, New York, one of the large cooperative agencies, is often called ecumenical. The Roman Catholic Church with headquarters at the Vatican, Vatican City, is an international church and its leaders regard it as universal or ecumenical.

EVANGELICAL. The term evangelical is variously used and defined in religious circles. It may refer to Protestants, compared to the Roman Catholic Church, as in Latin America. It may be used to designate individuals or churches that are especially active in evangelistic work. In Great Britain, the low church Anglican group, or school, is sometimes called evangelical. In America, the fundamentalists call themselves evangelical, meaning opposed to liberal Protestants. And certain liberal Protestants may deny that they are evangelical.

FEDERATED CHURCHES. Federated churches represent one form under which two or more churches in a community carry on their local activities in common, while each unit also maintains its denominational connection or allegiance. They are found mainly in villages throughout the United States. There is no complete statistical report on the extent of these churches, but 508 were reported in the Census of Religious Bodies, 1936, with 88,411 members. Four hundred twenty-six of these were in rural communities. Certain denominations were represented in these local federations more frequently than others. These were: Congregational Christian, Disciples of Christ, Methodist, Presbyterian, Baptist. It is believed that the first church of this type to be formed was in Massachusetts in 1887, and a large proportion are believed still to be in New England. There are relatively few in the Southern States. Each denominational unit adheres to the doctrine of the body with which it is affiliated, and makes its contribution to the benevolence program of the body. Usually Sunday schools are conducted in common. (CRB)

FUNDAMENTALISM. Many religious bodies designate their tenets as fundamental. A specific movement named Fundamentalist has been influential in the United States since about the year 1910. Thus there are now denominations (indeed, an unknown number) that call themselves fundamentalist. Fundamentalist literature opposes the critical study of the Scriptures, the "higher criticism"; it emphasizes the inerrancy and the verbal inspiration of the Bible; supports the virgin birth of Christ, His physical resurrection, His second coming, and His substitutionary atonement.

Controversy that must be labeled violent has stirred a number of denominations. This took the form of discussions between the fundamentalists and their opponents, who came to be known as modernists. Probably the Baptist and Presbyterian families of denominations were most affected, and certain local churches withdrew from these bodies and formed new denominations. The controversy goes on through special periodicals and agencies, but probably in the 1950's it affected the main large denominations less than in the 1930's. In other words, most of the large bodies had weathered their storms, and fundamentalists were solidly entrenched in their own denominations and special organizations.

A world organization of fundamentalists is The International Council of Christian Churches, Amsterdam, the Netherlands. National agencies in the United States that have local churches and denominations as constituencies are the national Association of Evangelicals, Chicago; and the American Council of Christian Churches, New York.

INDEPENDENT CHURCHES. There are single local churches in the United States not affiliated with any religious bodies. These are often called independent or union churches, but in many places they are also called community churches. They are expressions of a trend toward non-sectarian local unity. There is no complete enumeration of this group, but in 1936 the Census of Religious Bodies reported 384 with 40,276 members, of which 269 were in rural communities. At times an independent church decides to affiliate with a denomination. Thus the number of these churches is continually shifting. They are a group of churches concerning which no general statement about doctrine can be made. Each local unit decides for itself what doctrinal basis, if any, it shall have. Likewise all matters of form of organization are decided by the local church. Most of the 384 churches reporting to CRB conducted Sunday schools.

JEWISH-CHRISTIAN COOPERATION, *see above, Christian-Jewish Cooperation*

SUNDAY AND SABBATH SCHOOLS. Sunday and Sabbath schools are particularly emphasized by Protestant churches and Jewish congregations. The Roman Catholics rely on parochial schools for religious instruction of the young; they also arrange classes in parishes for religious instruction of those of their youth who attend public schools.

Sunday and Sabbath schools teach the Bible and many curriculums related thereto, give instruction in religion, and encourage their pupils to assume full membership in the congregation. They are thus known as institutions of enlistment for the parishes and congregations.

Sunday and Sabbath schools tend to rely on volunteer leadership, including teaching. They are thus often an expression of the initiative of lay persons, although often the clergyman exercises general supervision. In large parishes and congregations, professional directors of religious education are employed.

The first Sunday school was started in Gloucester, England, by Robert Raikes, in 1780. His motive was to give moral and religious training to the poor of the community. In this school the pupils were also taught to read. Because education was much needed, the idea spread. Everybody in the world would be taught to read the Bible. After a time the Sunday school was regarded as a means of teaching all young people everywhere, not alone the poor. Numerous associations of Sunday schools have been formed, and strong denominational boards and agencies prepare systematic curriculum materials and encourage improvement in methods.

There is a World Council of Christian Education and Sunday School Association with headquarters in London and New York. It reported over 40,000,000 members of Sunday and Sabbath schools in 1950, on all continents. Of these 3,500,000 were in England and Wales, 400,000 in Scotland, 130,000 in Ireland, 935,000 in Canada. In the U.S.A. in 1955 there was reported an enrollment of 38,-900,000 persons. (YBAC)

WOMEN IN THE MINISTRY. The ordination of women for the ministry is apparently most widely practiced by a group of Protestant denominations in the United States. The Bureau of the Census, Washington, reported that 6,777 women gave the ministry as their occupation in the population census of 1950. A study by the National Council of Churches of published reports indicated that sixty-five Protestant bodies ordain women and fourteen additional bodies ordain or license women. This includes such well-known bodies as the Presbyterian Church in the U.S.A., the Methodist Church, the Congregational Christian, Baptist, Disciples, Unitarian, and Universalist churches. Seven others gave women special status of some sort. (YBAC)

IV

GLOSSARY

The following glossary includes selected terms, being limited to those deemed by the author most necessary in a short book. In the process of presenting these definitions, note has been taken of the writings by officials of the religious bodies herein described, and of modern dictionaries.

Absolution: A rite of freeing from guilt and from punishment for sin, after confession, by a clergyman.

Adventist: A person or religious body believing that Christ will return to the earth; a believer in the "second coming."

Allah: In Islam, the name of the all-powerful God.

Anointing: The application of oil for the purpose of consecrating objects or persons; e.g., for completion of baptism, for promoting health, or preparation for death.

Apostolic: A doctrine or practice of or pertaining to the apostles, or to an apostle, named by Christ.

Apostolic succession: The theory of a continuing succession in the episcopacy and leadership of the churches, maintained from the apostolic to present times; emphasized in Eastern Orthodox, Roman Catholic, Anglican, and certain Protestant communions.

Arminian: The system of thought of, or the followers of, Arminius, a Dutch Protestant theologian (1560-1609) who denied certain of John Calvin's teachings and taught universal salvation.

Athanasian: The doctrine believed by Athanasius (293-373), defending the orthodox concepts of the divinity of Christ.

Atonement: The view that through the sufferings of Jesus Christ a sinner may be reconciled with God.

Autocephalous: The condition of being an independent head of a jurisdiction, as in the Eastern Orthodox churches.

Autonomous: Independent, or self-governing.

Baptism: An application of water to a person by immersion, sprinkling, or affusion, in a ceremonial, as a sign of removal of sin, and of admission into a Christian church. In a few Christian bodies baptism is of the spirit, by the Holy Spirit, and not with water.

Calvinist: A follower of John Calvin (1509-64). His teachings are summarized in prior articles.

Classis: In the Reformed bodies, a district association of churches consisting of all ministers and one layman from every local church, which supervises the local churches.

Communion: The ceremony of commemorating the death of Christ in the use of bread and wine as emblems of His flesh and blood; the various theologies related thereto are summarized under various bodies preceding, e.g., Lutheran, Roman Catholic, etc.

Confession: An admission of sin, on conversion, or to a clergyman; or a formulation of the beliefs of a religious body.

Confirmation: The ceremony whereby persons are admitted to a church; or a ratification of an action of a church group by a higher authority.

Congregational: A form of church organization in which there is no authority over the local congregation.

Creed: A formulation of the principal or fundamental beliefs of a religious body.

Dharma: In Buddhism and Hinduism, a term for that on which the law of truth and virtue is based; also used to designate the law of truth and virtue itself.

Doctrine: A teaching or a position of a religious body or of a theologian.

Dogma: A principle, or a system of principles, setting forth the teachings of a religious body.

Ecumenical: Universal, world-wide, general, or representing the whole Christian church.

Episcopal: A system of church government in which bishops have supervisory authority and other functions; or pertaining to or having to do with bishops.

Eucharist: The ceremony of commemorating the death of Christ in the use of bread and wine, as emblems of His flesh and blood; various theologies pertaining thereto are summarized in preceding accounts, e.g., Roman Catholic, Eastern Orthodox, Lutheran.

Evangelical: Indicating direct loyalty to the gospel of Christ; or, a group of churches alleging this emphasis in contrast to ecclesiastical systems or to rationalist religion; or, zeal for the Christian life as distinguished from ritual.

Ex-communication: An act or sentence of outlawing by a church of a person found guilty of practice or speech forbidden by the church.

Fundamentalist: A person holding to the infallibility of the Bible and other related teachings, believing they should be accepted literally.

Hierarchy: A system of government in which the rule is by the clergy; or, the arrangement of those governing the church, in order of their authority.

Holiness: A state of spiritual purity; or, persons designated for religious service.

Immaculate conception: The teaching that the Virgin Mary was conceived free of original sin.

Infallibility: A term applied to the teachings of the Pope of the Roman Catholic Church when he speaks under certain conditions on a matter of faith and morals; or, the teaching that the Scriptures are free of error.

Kharma: In Buddhism and Hinduism, an act of piety; or, the principle of causality, e.g., the moral causal sequence.

Liturgy: A form for public worship, as required, or as preferred; certain bodies which carry on uniform worship, in contrast to informal services, are called liturgical.

Mass: The principal service of worship of the Roman Catholic Church; also used by the high church party in the Anglican communion to designate the principal worship service.

Modernist: In contrast to a fundamentalist, a person who interprets the Bible in the light of modern scholarship and scientific knowledge.

Pentecostal: The experience of conversion consequent upon the descent of the Holy Ghost on the Disciples of Christ at the time of the Jewish Pentecost.

Predestinarian: A person or body believing that all events are determined by God, and that every one's eternal destiny is set by divine decree.

Presbytery: A church assembly in a body having the Presbyterian system of government, which has certain authority over the local congregations; or, used to designate a district with numerous local churches.

Sabbatarian: One who in belief and practice regards the seventh day (Saturday) as the Sabbath.

Sacrament: A religious rite possessing two parts: a physical sign and a spiritual good or result.

Salvation: The state of spiritual health; the rescue by God's power of a man from sin or guilt so that he may obtain blessedness.

Sanctification: The operation of the Holy Spirit enabling the believer to be led to holiness.

Second Coming: The return of Jesus Christ to the earth; see Adventist.

See: The place from which a bishop exercises his jurisdiction.

Synod: A church council or assembly, meeting at intervals, for exercise of those functions committed to it by the body or by the system of church government.

Trinitarian: A believer in the Trinity—that there is one divine nature, a union of Father, Son, and Holy Spirit; in most theologies a revelation which cannot be fully explained in words.

Unction: An anointing with oil in a ceremonial as of a person believed to be in danger of death.

Unitarian: A theology of the unity of God, denying the trinitarian concept, teaching the strict humanity of Jesus.

INDEX

INDEX

151

DUTTON PAPERBACKS

DUTTON PAPERBACKS